On the Witness Stand

Essays on Psychology and Crime

On the Witness Stand

Essays on Psychology and Crime

Hugo Munsterberg

with a new foreword by

Elizabeth Loftus

Classics in Psychology

Mark Hatala

series editor

Greentop Academic Press • Greentop, Missouri

On the Witness Stand: Essays on Psychology and Crime by Hugo
Munsterberg

ISBN-13: 978-1-933167-90-9
LCCN: 2009934683

Special thanks to Brianna Wagner, who was instrumental in putting
this volume together.

Series Editor: Mark Hatala, Ph.D.
Cover Design: Charles Dunbar
Composition: Age Positive Editorial Services

Table of Contents

Foreword

Foreword

I'm envious of Hugo Munsterberg. As a scientist born more than 80 years after him, I can only fantasize that a book of mine on eyewitness testimony might be reprinted 100 years after its initial publication. For Munsterberg this not only happened with his seminal book, *On the Witness Stand*, but an entire issue of the journal Applied Cognitive Psychology (ACP) was devoted to him to celebrate the centennial of the publication of that groundbreaking work. I thought I knew a lot about Munsterberg's life and work, but I learned a great deal more from reading the fine contributions in the ACP special issue.

I first read *On the Witness Stand* in the 1970's when preparing to write my first book on eyewitness testimony. I devoted several pages to his description of a dramatic but helter-skelter experiment in which an incident is staged in a classroom, and later the students had to recount what they saw. Mistakes were common. "Words were put into the mouths of men who had been silent spectators…; actions were attributed to chief participants of which not the slightest trace existed." However, Munsterberg's book was very controversial in its time. A year after *On the Witness Stand* was published, John Henry Wigmore wrote a wonderfully satirical attack on the book. It was constructed in the form of a trial in which the members of the bar sued Munsterberg for defamation. Plaintiffs took issue with Munsterberg's claims that psychological methods for testing the accuracy of testimony were superior to those being used in American courts. After the briefest of deliberations, the jury found for the plaintiffs and awarded them damages of one dollar.

Of course the trial never happened and the satirical nature of the article is made even more clear when the readers learn that the case took place on April Fools Day, and a Mr. X. Perry Ment was one of Munsterberg's defense lawyers. Wigmore had put Munsterberg on trial in an imaginary courtroom in an article that attorney James Doyle noted is remembered as a "savage, bloodthirsty slaughter of psychology (and) psychologists...." (See Doyle's terrific book *True Witness*). Given how genial a tone Munsterberg actually adopted, this savage response is somewhat unexpected.

Who was Hugo Munsterberg? He was a Professor of Psychology at Harvard when he wrote his famous book. Widely touted as the founder of the discipline of psychology and law, his book is often considered a significant moment for the founding of that field. Although other researchers had published important work before Munsterberg (such as George Frederick Arnold and William Stern), he achieved more fame. Munsterberg was born in 1863, the same year that the fire extinguisher was patented, Abraham Lincoln signed the Emancipation Proclamation, and the American Civil War was raging. Born to an affluent family, Munsterberg studied psychology at the University of Leipzig under the supervision of Wilhelm Wundt and went on to earn an MD degree from the University of Heidelberg. He landed the Harvard position, succeeding William James, who had been running the psychology laboratory. But fame came his way in part because he wrote frequently for a wide popular audience of readers, as well as for other academics.

Munsterberg's book introduced the public to many ideas that are still central to the field of eyewitness testimony. He showed us how error prone witnesses can be. He attacked the assumptions of the legal systems about protections against witness error, such as the ability to rely on witness demeanor or confidence. He urged the legal field to listen to the messages of experimental psychology. Munsterberg might be surprised to know that today many juries are listening to the messages of experimental psychology, through the testimony of expert witnesses. Of course, one criticism of such testimony is that the basic research is based on groups of subjects, and that research often shows that a group that witnesses an event under one condition performs better than a group that witnesses that event under a different condition (for example, long exposures to an event versus very brief exposures). But how do we apply this to a single specific case? This criticism is closely related to the "one-legged, six-toed Scotsman" criticism, described so aptly in the ACP special issue: The witness in the case at bar is a one-legged, six-toed Scotsman. There is not a single experiment out there in which even one of the subjects was a one-legged, six-toed Scotsman. So how do these studies apply? One answer, of course, is that the number of legs, or toes, or even the Scottish background, are not relevant to understanding the impact of the variable of interest. We may not have a study involving people exactly like the party in the case but we often have an excellent theory combined with prior research to guide our understanding. If you know that a bullet shot through a brain leads to death when shot in a parking lot, a restaurant, or a rowdy bar, you may not need a special study to show that it will also lead to death if shot through the brain in a bowling alley.

Munsterberg would undoubtedly be pleased with the progress made by the scientists who stood on his shoulders. The ACP special issue describes progress in our understanding of the relationship between accuracy and confidence, the effects of the retention interval, and the effects of heightened stress, among other issues. Munsterberg would be interested to learn of some recent innovative efforts to study the effects of heightened stress on witness memory. One research group has been studying memory in a group of soldiers who are being trained in techniques to avoid capture and to survive imprisonment as a prisoner of war. The training occurs at the SERE School (for Survival, Evasion, Resistance & Escape). One purpose of the training is to psychologically prepare soldiers for the eventuality of being captured by the enemy forces. It is extremely stressful for participants. Quang X. Pham wrote about his experiences in his fine memoir *A Sense of Duty*. He describes arriving at the mock prison greeted by singsong Arabic music blasting through loudspeakers. Sandbags were placed over his head and he was forced to crawl on his knees to a prison cell that resembled a dog kennel. He was slammed against the wall. He was slapped many times, until stars appeared in his vision. He bit his gums and his mouth filled with blood. He was subjected to the infamous waterboard torture. He spent one night drenched in his own piss after accidentally kicking over his urine bowl. Concluding his story, he remarked: "I left SERE school a few pounds lighter, with a swollen mouth and an incredible fear of being captured by the enemy."

A research team headed by psychiatrist Charles Morgan used the SERE school to study the memories of these soldiers for their SERE experiences. He tested them after their ordeal and found that they made huge mistakes of recollection, including their identification of the captor who had conducted the horrendous interrogation. Moreover, despite whatever training and physical health they may have possessed when they entered the school, the soldiers were highly susceptible to having their recollections contaminated with misinformation. So much for the widely-held lay view that extremely stressful events create an imprint in the brain and are recallable in pristine form.

Munsterberg died in 1916, the same year that the light switch was invented, U.S. President Woodrow Wilson signed a bill incorporating the Boy Scouts of America, Margaret Sanger opened the first U.S. birth control clinic (a forerunner of Planned Parenthood), and World War One was raging. He contributed his own "fire extinguisher" and "light switch" in terms of a legacy to psychology that lives on in forms that he would be proud of. His successors have made huge empirical generalizations and developed useful theoretical accounts of the phenomena he first described 100 years ago.

Elizabeth Loftus, Ph.D.

Distinguished Professor
Psychology & Social Behavior
Criminology, Law & Society
Cognitive Sciences
School of Law

University of California, Irvine

1
Introduction

There are about fifty psychological laboratories in the United States alone. The average educated man has hitherto not noticed this. If he chances to hear of such places, he fancies that they serve for mental healing, or telepathic mysteries, or spiritistic performances. What else can a laboratory have to do with the mind? Has not the soul been for two thousand years the domain of the philosopher? What has psychology to do with electric batteries and intricate machines? Too often have I read such questions in the faces of visiting friends who came to the Harvard Psychological Laboratory in Emerson Hall and found, with surprise, twenty-seven rooms overspun with electric wires and filled with chronoscopes and kymographs and tachistoscopes and ergographs, and a mechanic busy at his work.

The development of this new science could remain unnoticed because it was such a rapid one, surprising in its extent even to those who started it. When, as a young student, I went to the University of Leipzig in the eighties of the last century, the little psychological laboratory there, founded by Professor Wundt, was still the only one in the world. No Western country college would to-day be satisfied with those poor little rooms in which the master of the craft made his experiments with his few students. But since that time the Leipzig workshop has been steadily growing, and every year has seen the foundation of new institutes by the pupils of Wundt, and later by their pupils. The first German laboratory outside of Leipzig was the one which I founded in Freiburg just twenty years ago. At about the same time Stanley Hall and Cattell brought the work from Leipzig over the ocean. Today there exists hardly a university which has not opened a workshop for this youngest of the natural sciences.

But more brilliant than the external expansion has been the inner growth. If the new science started in poor quarters, it was still more modest at the beginning in its outlook toward the work. Experimental psychology did not even start with experiments of its own; it rather took its problems at first from the neighbouring sciences. There was the physiologist or the physician who made careful experiments on the functions of the eye and the ear and the skin and the muscles, and who got in this way somewhat as by-products interesting experimental results on seeing and hearing and touching and acting; and yet all these by-products evidently had psychological importance. Or there was the physicist who had to make experiments to find out how far our human senses can furnish us an exact knowledge of the outer world; and again his results could not but be of importance for the psychology of perception. Or there was perhaps the astronomer who was bothered with his "personal equation," as he was alarmed to find that it took different astronomers different times to register the passing of a star. The astronomers had, therefore, in the interest of their calculations, to make experiments to find out with what rapidity an impression is noticed and reacted upon. But this again was an experimental result which evidently concerned, first of all, the student of mental life.

In this way all kinds of scientists who cared little for psychology had gathered the most various psychological results with experimental methods, and the psychologists saw that they could not afford to ignore such results of natural science. It would not do to go on claiming, for instance, that thought is quick as lightning when the experiments of the astronomers had proved that even the simplest mental act is a slow process, the time of which can be measured. Experimental psychology, therefore, started with an effort to repeat on its own account and from its own point of view those researches which others had performed. But it seemed evident that this kind of work would never yield more than some little facts in the periphery of mental life — borderland facts between mind and body. No one dreamed of the possibility of carrying such experimental method to the higher problems of inner life which seemed the exclusive region of the philosophising psychologist. But as soon as experimental psychology began to work in its own workshops, it was most natural to carry the new method persistently to new and ever new groups of problems. The tools of experiment were now systematically used for the study of memory and the connection of ideas, then of attention and of imagination, of space perception and time sense; slowly they became directed to the problems of feeling and emotion, of impulse and volition, of imitation and reasoning. Groups of mental functions which yesterday seemed beyond the reach of experimental laboratory methods, to-day appear quite accessible. It may be said that there is now hardly a corner of mental life into which experimental psychology has not thrown its searchlight.

It may seem strange that this whole wonderful development should have gone on in complete detachment from the problems of practical life. Considering that perception and memory, feeling and emotion, attention and volition, and so on, are the chief factors of our daily life, entering into every one of our enjoyments and duties, experiences and professions, it seems astonishing that no path led from the seclusion of the psychological workshop to the market-place of the world.

Of course this separation was no disadvantage to psychology. It is never a gain when a science begins too early to look aside to practical needs. The longer a discipline can develop itself under the single influence, the search for pure truth, the more solid will be its foundations. But now experimental psychology has reached a stage at which it seems natural and sound to give attention also to its possible service for the practical needs of life.

This must not be misunderstood. To make psychology serviceable cannot mean simply to pick up some bits of theoretical psychology and to throw them down before the public. Just this has sometimes been done by amateurish hands and with disastrous results. Undigested psychological knowledge has been in the past recklessly forced on helpless schoolteachers, and in educational meetings the blackboards were at one time filled with drawings of ganglion cells and tables of reaction-times. No warning against such "yellow psychology" can be serious enough.

If experimental psychology is to enter into its period of practical service, it cannot be a question of simply using the ready-made results for ends which were not in view during the experiments. What is needed is to adjust research to the practical problems themselves and thus, for instance, when education is in question, to start psychological experiments directly from educational problems. Applied Psychology will then become an independent experimental science which stands related to the ordinary experimental psychology as engineering to physics.

The time for such Applied Psychology is surely near, and work has been started from most various sides. Those fields of practical life which come first in question may be said to be education, medicine, art, economics, and law. The educator will certainly not resist the suggestion that systematic experiments on memory or attention, for instance, can be useful for his pedagogical efforts. The physician to-day doubts still less that he can be aided in the understanding of nervous and mental diseases, or in the understanding of pain and of mental factors in treatment, by the psychological studies of the laboratory. It is also not difficult to convince the artist that his instinctive creation may well be supplemented by the psychologist's study of colour and form, of rhythm and harmony, of suggestion and aesthetic emotion. And even the business world begins to understand that the effectiveness of economic life depends in a thousand forms on factors for which the student of psychology is a real specialist. His experiments can indicate best how the energies of mill-hands can reach the best results, and how advertisements ought to be shaped, and what belongs to ideal salesmanship. And experience shows that the politician who wants to know and to master minds, the naturalist who needs to use his mind in the service of discovery, the officer who wants to keep up discipline, and the minister who wants to open minds to inspiration — all are ready to see that certain chapters of Applied Psychology are sources of help and strength for them. The lawyer alone is obdurate.

The lawyer and the judge and the juryman are sure that they do not need the experimental psychologist. They do not wish to see that in this field preëminently applied experimental psychology has made strong strides, led by Binet, Stern, Lipmann, Jung, Wertheimer, Gross, Sommer, Aschaffenburg, and other scholars. They go on thinking that their legal instinct and their common sense supplies them with all that is needed and somewhat more; and if the time is ever to come when even the jurist is to show some concession to the spirit of modern psychology, public opinion will have to exert some pressure. Just in the line of the law it therefore seems necessary not to rely simply on the technical statements of scholarly treatises, but to carry the discussion in the most popular form possible before the wider tribunal of the general reader.

With this aim in mind — while working at a treatise on "Applied Psychology," which is to cover the whole ground with technical detail — I have written the following popular sketches, which select only a few problems in which psychology and law come in contact. They deal essentially with the mind of the witness on the witness stand; only the last, on the prevention of crime, takes another direction. I have not touched so far the psychology of the attorney, of the judge, or of the jury — problems which lend themselves to very interesting experimental treatment. Even the psychology of the witness is treated in no way exhaustively; my only purpose is to turn the attention of serious men to an absurdly neglected field which demands the full attention of the social community.

2

Illusions

There had been an automobile accident. Before the court one of the witnesses, who had sworn to tell "the whole truth, and nothing but the truth," declared that the entire road was dry and dusty; the other swore that it had rained and the road was muddy. The one said that the automobile was running very slowly; the other, that he had never seen an automobile rushing more rapidly. The first swore that there were only two or three people on the village road; the other, that a large number of men, women, and children were passing by. Both witnesses were highly respectable gentlemen, neither of whom had the slightest interest in changing the facts as he remembered them.

I find among my notes another case, where everything depended upon the time which had passed between a whistle signal from the street and the noise of an explosion. It was of the greatest importance for the court to know whether the time was long enough to walk a certain distance for which at least half a minute was needed. Of two unbiassed witnesses, one swore that the time was less than ten seconds; the other that it was more than one minute. Again, there was a case where it was essential to find out whether at a certain riot the number of guests in the hall was larger than the forty who had been invited to attend. There were witnesses who insisted that there could not have been more than twenty persons present, and others who were sure that they saw more than one hundred. In a case of poisoning, some members of the family testified that the beverage had a disagreeable, sour taste, others, that it was tasteless, and others, that it was sweet. In some Bowery wrangle, one witness was quite certain that a rowdy had taken a beer-mug and kept it in his fist while he beat with it the skull of his comrade; while others saw that the two were separated by a long table, and that the assailant used the mug as a missile, throwing it a distance of six or eight feet. In another trial, one witness noticed at the sea-shore in moonlight a woman with a child, while another witness was not less sure that it was a man with a dog. And only recently passengers in a train which passed a courtyard were sure, and swore, that they had taken in at a glance the distinct picture of a man whipping a child; one swore that he had a clean-shaven face, a hat, and was standing, while another swore that he had a full beard, no hat, and was sitting on a bench. The other day two most reliable expert shorthand writers felt sure that they had heard the utterances which they wrote down, and yet the records differed widely in important points.

There is no need of heaping up such illustrations from actual cases, as everyone who remembers the last half-dozen murder trials of his city knows with what regularity these differences in reports of witnesses occur. We may abstract from all cases which demand technical knowledge; we want to speak here only of direct observations and of impressions which do not need any special acquaintance with the matter. Wherever real professional knowledge is needed, the door is, of course, open to every variety of opinion, and one famous expert may conscientiously contradict the other. No, we speak here only of those impressions for which every layman is prepared and where there can be no difference of opinion. We further abstract entirely from all cases of intentional deception; the witness who lies offers no psychological interest for the student of illusions. And we exclude all questions of mental disease. Thus there remain the unintentional mistakes of the sound mind, — and the psychologist must ask at once, Are they all of the same order? Is it enough to label them simply as illusions of memory.

To make memory responsible is indeed the routine way. It is generally taken for granted that we all perceive our surroundings uniformly. In case there were only twenty men in the hall, no one could have seen one hundred. In case the road was muddy, no one can have seen it dusty. In case the man was shaved, no one can have seen the beard. If there is still disagreement, it must have crept in through the trickery of memory. The perception must be correct; its later reproduction may be false. But do we really all perceive the same thing, and does it have the same meaning to us in our immediated absorption of the surrounding world? Is the court sufficiently aware of the great differences between men's perceptions, and does the court take sufficient trouble to examine the capacities and habits with which the witness moves through the world which he believes he observes? Of course some kind of a "common-sense" consideration has entered, consciously or unconsciously, into hundreds of judicial decisions, inasmuch as the contradictory evidence has to be sifted. The judges have on such occasions more or less boldly philosophised or psychologised on their own account; but to consult the psychological authorities was out of the question. Legal theorists have even proudly boasted of the fact that the judges always found their way without psychological advice, and yet the records of such cases, for instance, in railroad damages, quickly show that the psychological inspirations of the bench are often directly the opposite of demonstrable facts. To be sure, the judge may bolster up the case with preceding decisions, but even if the old decision was justified, is such an amateur psychologist prepared to decide whether the mental situation is really the same in the new case? Such judicial self-help was unavoidable as long as the psychology of earlier times was hazy and vague but all that has changed with the exact character of the new psychology.

The study of these powers no longer lies outside of the realm of science. The progress of experimental psychology makes it an absurd incongruity that the State should devote its fullest energy to the clearing up of all the physical happenings, but should never ask the psychological expert to determine the value of that factor which becomes most influential — the mind of the witness. The demand that the memory of the witness should be tested with the methods of modern psychology has been raised sometimes, but it seems necessary to add that the study of his perceptive judgment will have to find its way into the court-room, too.

Last winter I made, quite by the way, a little experiment with the students of my regular psychology course in Harvard. Several hundred young men, mostly between twenty and twenty-three, took part. It was a test of a very trivial sort. I asked them simply, without any theoretical introduction, at the beginning of an ordinary lecture, to write down careful answers to a number of questions referring to that which they would see or hear. I urged them to do it as conscientiously and carefully as possible, and the hundreds of answers which I received showed clearly that every one had done his best. I shall confine my report to the first hundred papers taken up at random. At first I showed them a large sheet of white cardboard on which fifty little black squares were pasted in irregular order. I exposed it for five seconds, and asked them how many black spots were on the sheet. The answers varied between twenty-five and two hundred. The answer, over one hundred, was more frequent than that of below fifty. Only three felt unable to give a definite reply. Then I showed a cardboard which contained only twenty such spots. This time the replies ran up to seventy and down to ten. We had here highly trained, careful observers, whose attention was concentrated on the material, and who had full time for quiet scrutiny. Yet in both cases there were some who believed that they saw seven or eight times more points than some others saw; and yet we should be disinclined to believe in the sincerity of two witnesses, of whom one felt sure that he saw two hundred persons in a hall in which the other found only twenty-five.

My next question referred to the perception of time. I asked the students to give the number of seconds which passed between two loud clicks. I separated the two clicks at first by ten seconds, and in a further experiment by three seconds. When the distance was ten, the answers varied between half a second and sixty seconds, a good number judging forty-five seconds as the right time. The one who called it half a second was a Chinese, while all those whose judgments ranged from one second to sixty seconds were average Americans. When the objective time was three seconds, the answers varied between half a second and fifteen seconds. I emphasise that these large fluctuations showed themselves in spite of the fact that the students knew beforehand that they were to estimate the time interval. The variations would probably have been still greater if the question had been put to them after hearing the sound without previous information; and yet a district attorney hopes for a reliable reply when he inquires of a witness, perhaps of a cabman, how much time passed by between a cry and the shooting in the cab.

In my third experiment I wanted to find out how rapidity is

estimated. I had on the platform a large clock with a white dial over which one black pointer moved once around in five seconds. The end of the black pointer, which had the form of an arrow, moved over the edge of the dial with a velocity of ten centimeters in one second; that is, in one second the arrow moved through a space of about a finger's length. Now, I made this clock go for a whole minute, and asked the observers to watch carefully the rapidity of the arrow, and to describe, either in figures or by comparisons with moving objects, the speed with which that arrow moved along. Most men preferred comparisons with other objects. The list begins as follows: man walking slowly; accommodation-train; bicycle-rider; funeral cortège in a city street; trotting dog; faster than trot of man; electric car; express train; goldfish in water; fastest automobile speed; very slowly, like a snail; lively spider; and so on. Would it seem possible that university students, trained in observation, could watch a movement constantly through a whole minute, and yet disagree whether it moved as slowly as a snail or as rapidly as an express-train. And yet it is evident that the form of the experiment excluded every possible mistake of memory and excluded every suggestive influence. The observation was made deliberately and without haste. Those who judged in figures showed not less variation. The list begins: one revolution in two seconds; one revolution in forty-five seconds; three inches a second; twelve feet a second; thirty seconds to the hundred yards; seven miles an hour; fifteen miles an hour; forty miles an hour; and so on. In reality the arrow would have moved in an hour about a third of a mile. Not a few of the judgments, therefore, multiplied the speed by more than one hundred.

In my next test I asked the class to describe the sound they would hear and to say from what source it came. The sound which

I produced was the tone of a large tuning-fork, which I struck with a little hammer below the desk, invisibly to the students. Among the hundred students whose papers I examined for this record were exactly two who recognised it as a tuning-fork tone. All the other judgments took it for a bell, or an organ-pipe, or a muffled gong, or a brazen instrument, or a horn, or a cello string, or a violin, and so on. Or they compared it with as different noises as the growl of a lion, a steam whistle, a fog-horn, a fly-wheel, a human song, and what not. The description, on the other hand, called it: soft, mellow, humming, deep, dull, solemn, resonant, penetrating, full, rumbling, clear, low; but then again, rough, sharp, whistling, and so on. Again I insist that every one knew beforehand that he was to observe the tone, which I announced by a signal. How much more would the judgments have differed if the tone had come in unexpectedly? — a tone which even now appeared so soft to some and so rough to others — like a bell to one and like a whistle to his neighbour.

I turn to a few experiments in which I showed several sheets of white cardboard, of which each contained a variety of dark and light ink-spots in a somewhat fantastic arrangement. Each of these cards was shown for two seconds, and it was suggested that these rough ink-drawings represented something in the outer world. Immediately after seeing one, the students were to write down what the drawing represented. In some cases the subjects remained sceptical and declared that those spots did not represent anything, but were merely blots of ink. In the larger number the suggestion was effective, and a definite object was recognised. The list of answers for one picture begins: soldiers in a valley; grapes; a palace; river-bank; Japanese landscape; foliage; rabbit; woodland scene; town with towers; rising storm; shore of lake; garden; flags;

men in landscape; hair in curling-papers; china plate; war picture; country square; lake in a jungle; trees with stone wall; clouds; harvest scene; elephant; map; lake with castle in background; trees; and so on. The list of votes for the next picture, which had finer details, started with: spider; landscape; turtle; butterfly; woman's head; bunch of war-flags; ballet-dancers; crowd of people; cactus plant; skunk going down a log; centipede; boat on pond; crow's nest beetle; flower; island; and so forth. There are hardly any repetitions, with the exception that the vague term "landscape" occurs often. Of course, we know, since the days of Hamlet and Polonius, that a cloud can look like a camel and like a whale. And yet such an abundance of variations was hardly to be foreseen.

My next question did not refer to immediate perception, but to a memory image so vividly at every one's disposal that I assumed a right to substitute it directly for a perception. I asked my men to compare the apparent size of the full moon to that of some object held in the hand at arm's length. I explained the question carefully, and said that they were to describe an object just large enough, when seen at arm's length, to cover the whole full moon. My list of answers begins as follows: quarter of a dollar; fair-sized canteloupe; at the horizon, large dinner plate, overhead, dessert-plate; my watch; six inches in diameter; silver dollar; hundred times as large as my watch; man's head; fifty-cent piece; nine inches in diameter; grape-fruit; carriage-wheel; butter-plate; orange; ten feet; two inches; one-cent piece; school-room clock; a pea; soup-plate; fountain-pen; lemon-pie; palm of the hand; three feet in diameter: enough to show, again, the overwhelming manifoldness of the impressions received. To the surprise of my readers, perhaps, it may be added at once that the only man who was right was the one who compared it to a pea. It is most probable that the results would not have been different if I had asked the question on a moonlight night with the full moon overhead. The substitution of the memory image for the immediate perception can hardly have impaired the correctness of the judgments. If in any court the size of a distant object were to be given by witnesses, and one man declared it appeared as large as a pea at arm's distance, and the second as large as a lemon-pie and the third ten feet in diameter, it would hardly be fair to form an objective judgment till the psychologist had found out which mental factors were entering into that estimate.

There were many more experiments in the list; but as I want to avoid all technicality, I refer to only two more, which are somewhat related. First, I showed to the men some pairs of coloured paper squares, and they had ample time to write down which of the two appeared to them darker. At first it was a red and a blue; then a blue and a green; and finally a blue and a grey. My interest was engaged entirely with the last pair. The grey was objectively far lighter than the dark blue, and any one with an unbiassed mind who looked at those two squares of paper could have not the slightest doubt that the blue was darker. Yet about one-fifth of the men wrote that the grey was darker.

Now, let us keep this in mind in looking over the last experiment, which I want to report. I stood on the platform behind a low desk and begged the men to watch and to describe everything which I was going to do from one given signal to another. As soon as the signal was given, I lifted with my right hand a little revolving wheel with a colour-disk and made it run and change its color, and all the time, while I kept the little instrument at the height of my head, I turned my eyes eagerly toward it. While this was going on, up to the closing signal, I took with my left hand, at first, a pencil

from my vest-pocket and wrote something at the desk; then I took
my watch out and laid it on the table; then I took a silver cigarette-
box from my pocket, opened it, took a cigarette out of it, closed it
with a loud click, and returned it to my pocket; and then came the
ending signal. The results showed that eighteen of the hundred
had not noticed anything of all that I was doing with my left hand.
Pencil and watch and cigarettes had simply not existed for them.
The mere fact that I myself seemed to give all my attention to the
colour-wheel had evidently inhibited in them the impressions of
the other side. Yet I had made my movements of the left arm so
ostentatiously, and I had beforehand so earnestly insisted that they
ought to watch every single movement, that I hardly expected to
make any one overlook the larger part of my actions. It showed
that the medium, famous for her slate tricks, was right when she
asserted that as soon as she succeeded in turning the attention
of her client to the slate in her hand, he would not notice if an
elephant should pass behind her through the room.

But the chief interest belongs to the surprising fact that of
those eighteen men, fourteen were the same who, in the foregoing
experiment, judged the light grey to be darker than the dark
blue. That coincidence was, of course, not chance. In the case
of the darkness experiment the mere idea of greyness gave to
their suggestible minds the belief that the colourless grey must be
darker than any colour. They evidently did not judge at all from
the optical impression, but entirely from their conception of grey
as darkness. The coincidence, therefore, proved clearly how very
quickly a little experiment such as this with a piece of blue and
grey paper, which can be performed in a few seconds, can pick out
for us those minds which are probably unfit to report, whether
an action has been performed in their presence or not. Whatever

they expect to see they do see; and if the attention is turned in one direction, they are blind and deaf and idiotic in the other.

Enough of my class-room experiments. Might they not indeed work as a warning against the blind confidence in the observations of the average normal man, and might they not reinforce the demand for a more careful study of the individual differences between those on the witness stand? Of course, such study would be one-sided if the psychologist were only to emphasise the varieties of men and the differences by which one man's judgment and observation may be counted on to throw out an opposite report from that of another man. No, the psychologist in the court-room should certainly give not less attention to the analysis of those illusions which are common to all men and of which as yet common sense knows too little. The jurymen and the judge do not discriminate, whether the witness tells that he saw in late twilight a woman in a red gown or one in a blue gown. They are not expected to know that such a faint light would still allow the blue colour sensation to come in, while the red colour sensation would have disappeared.

They are not obliged to know what directions of sound are mixed up by all of us and what are discriminated; they do not know, perhaps, that we can never be in doubt whether we heard on the country road a cry from the right or from the left, but we may be utterly unable to say whether we heard it from in front or from behind. They have no reason to know that the victim of a crime may have been utterly unable to perceive that he was stabbed with a pointed dagger; he may have felt it like a dull blow. We hear the witnesses talking about the taste of poisoned liquids, and there is probably no one in the jury-box who knows enough of physiological psychology to be aware that the same substance may taste quite differently on different parts of the tongue. We may hear quarrelling parties in a civil suit testify as to the size and length and form of a field as it appeared to them, and yet there is no one to remind the court that the same distance must appear quite differently under a hundred different conditions. The judge listens, perhaps, to a description of things which the witness has secretly seen through the keyhole of the door; he does not understand why all the judgments as to the size of objects and their place are probably erroneous under such circumstances. The witness may be sure of having felt something wet, and yet he may have felt only some smooth, cold metal. In short, every chapter and sub-chapter of sense psychology may help to clear up the chaos and the confusion which prevail in the observation of witnesses.

But, as we have insisted, it is never a question of pure sense perception. Associations, judgments, suggestions, penetrate into every one of our observations. We know from the drawings of children how they believe that they see all that they know really exists; and so do we ourselves believe that we perceive at least all that we expect. I remember some experiments in my laboratory where I showed printed words with an instantaneous illumination. Whenever I spoke a sentence before-hand, I was able to influence the seeing of the word. The printed word was courage: I said something about the university life, and the subject read the word as college. The printed word was Philistines: I, apparently without intention, had said something about colonial policy, and my subject read Philippines. In this way, of course, the fraudulent advertisement makes us overlook some essential element which may change the meaning of the offer entirely. Experimental psychology has at last cleared the ground, and to ignore this whole science and to be satisfied with the primitive psychology of common sense seems really out of order when crime and punishment are in question and the analysis of the mind of the witness might change the whole aspect of the case.

It is enough if we have to suffer from these mental varieties in our daily life; at least the court-room ought to come nearer to the truth, and ought to show the way. The other organs of society may then slowly follow. It may be that, ultimately, even the newspapers may learn then from the legal practice, and may take care that their witnesses be examined, too, as to their capacity of observation. Those experiments described from my class-room recommend at least mildness of judgment when we compare the newspaper reports with each other. Since I saw that my own students do not know whether a point moves with the slowness of a snail or with the rapidity of an express-train; whether a time interval is half a second or a whole minute; whether there are twenty-five points or two hundred; whether a tone comes from a whistle, a gong, or a violin; whether the moon is small as a pea or large as a man, — I am not surprised any more when I read the reports of the papers.

I had occasion recently to make an address on peace in New York before a large gathering, to which there was an unexpected and somewhat spirited reply. The reporters sat immediately in front of the platform. One man wrote that the audience was so surprised by my speech that it received it in complete silence; another wrote that I was constantly interrupted by loud applause, and that at the end of my address the applause continued for minutes. The one wrote that during my opponent's speech I was constantly smiling; the other noticed that my face remained grave and without a smile. The one said that I grew purple-red from excitement; and the other found that I grew white like chalk. The one told us that my critic, while speaking, walked up and down the large stage; and the other, that he stood all the while at my side and patted me in a fatherly way on the shoulder. And Mr. Dooley finally heard that before I made my speech on peace I was introduced as the Professor from the Harvard War School — but it may be that Mr. Dooley was not himself present.

3
The Memory of the Witness

Last summer I had to face a jury as witness in a trial. While I was with my family at the seashore my city house had been burglarised and I was called upon to give an account of my findings against the culprit whom they had caught with a part of the booty. I reported under oath that the burglars had entered through a cellar window, and then described what rooms they had visited. To prove, in answer to a direct question, that they had been there at night, I told that I had found drops of candle wax on the second floor. To show that they intended to return, I reported that they had left a large mantel clock, packed in wrapping paper, on the dining-room table. Finally, as to the amount of clothes which they had taken, I asserted that the burglars did not get more than a specified list which I had given the police.

Only a few days later I found that every one of these statements was wrong. They had not entered through the window, but had broken the lock of the cellar door; the clock was not packed by them in wrapping paper, but in a tablecloth; the candle droppings were not on the second floor, but in the attic; the list of lost garments was to be increased by seven more pieces; and while my story under oath spoke always of two burglars, I do not know that there was more than one. How did all those mistakes occur? I have no right to excuse myself on the plea of a bad memory. During the last eighteen years I have delivered about three thousand university lectures. For those three thousand coherent addresses I had not once a single written or printed line or any notes whatever on the platform; and yet there has never been a moment when I have had to stop for a name or for the connection of the thought. My memory serves me therefore rather generously. I stood there, also, without prejudice against the defendant. Inasmuch as he expects to spend the next twelve years at a place of residence where he will have little chance to read my writings, I may confess frankly that I liked the man. I was thus under the most favourable conditions for speaking the whole truth and nothing but the truth, and, as there is probably no need for the assurance of my best intentions, I felt myself somewhat alarmed in seeing how many illusions had come in.

Of course, I had not made any careful examination of the house. I had rushed in from the seashore as soon as the police notified me, in the fear that valuable contents of the house might have been destroyed or plundered. When I saw that they had treated me mildly, inasmuch as they had started in the wine cellar and had forgotten under its genial influence, on the whole, what they had come for, I had taken only a superficial survey. That a clock was lying on the table, packed ready to be taken away, had impressed itself clearly on my memory; but that it was packed in a tablecloth had made evidently too slight an impression on my consciousness. My imagination gradually substituted the more usual method of packing with wrapping paper, and I was ready to take an oath on it until I went back later, at the end of the summer vacation. In the same way I got a vivid image of the candle droppings on the floor, but as, at the moment of the perception, no interest was attached to the peculiar place where I saw them, I slowly substituted in my memory the second floor for the attic, knowing surely from strewn papers and other disorder that they had ransacked both places.

As to the clothes, I had simply forgotten that I had put several suits in a remote wardrobe; only later did I find it empty. My other two blunders clearly arose under the influence of suggestion. The police and every one about the house had always taken as a matter of course that the entrance was made by a cellar window, as it would have been much more difficult to use the locked doors. I had thus never examined the other hypothesis, and yet it was found later that they did succeed in removing the lock of a door. And finally, my whole story under oath referred to two burglars, without any doubt at the moment. The fact is, they had caught the gentleman in question when he, a few days later, plundered another house. He then shot a policeman, but was arrested, and in his room they found a jacket with my name written in it by the tailor. That alone gave a hint that my house also had been entered; but from the first moment he insisted that there had been two in this burglary and that the other man had the remainder of the booty. The other has not been found, and he probably still wears my badges; but I never heard any doubt as to his existence, and thus, in mere imitation, I never doubted that there was a companion, in spite of the fact that every part of the performance might just as well have been carried out by one man alone; and, after all, it is not impossible that he should lie as well as shoot and steal.

In this way, in spite of my best intentions, in spite of good memory and calm mood, a whole series of confusions, of illusions, of forgetting, of wrong conclusions, and of yielding to suggestions were mingled with what I had to report under oath, and my only consolation is the fact that in a thousand courts at a thousand places all over the world, witnesses every day affirm by oath in exactly the same way much worse mixtures of truth and untruth, combinations of memory and of illusion, of knowledge and of suggestion, of experience and wrong conclusions. Not one of my mistakes was of the slightest consequence. But is it probable that this is always so? Is it not more natural to suppose that every day errors creep into the work of justice through wrong evidence which has the outer marks of truth and trust-worthiness? Of course, judge and jury and, later, the newspaper reader try their best to weigh the evidence. Not every sworn statement is accepted as absolute reality. Contradictions between witnesses are too familiar. But the instinctive doubt refers primarily to veracity. The public in the main suspects that the witness lies, while taking for granted that if he is normal and conscious of responsibility he may forget a thing, but it would not believe that he could remember the wrong thing. The confidence in the reliability of memory is so general that the suspicion of memory illusions evidently plays a small rôle in the mind of the juryman, and even the cross-examining lawyer is mostly dominated by the idea that a false statement is the product of intentional falsehood.

All this is a popular illusion against which modern psychology must seriously protest. Justice would less often miscarry if all who are to weigh evidence were more conscious of the treachery of human memory. Yes, it can be said that, while the court makes the fullest use of all the modern scientific methods when, for instance, a drop of dried blood is to be examined in a murder case, the same court is completely satisfied with the most unscientific and haphazard methods of common prejudice and ignorance when a mental product, especially the memory report of a witness, is to be examined. No juryman would be expected to follow his general impressions in the question as to whether the blood on the murderer's shirt is human or animal. But he is expected to make up his mind as to whether the memory ideas of a witness are objective reproductions of earlier experience or are mixed up with associations and suggestions. The court proceeds as if the physiological chemistry of blood examination had made wonderful progress, while experimental psychology, with its efforts to analyse the mental faculties, still stood where it stood two thousand years ago.

The fact is that experimental psychology has not only in general experienced a wonderful progress during the last decades, but has also given in recent years an unusual amount of attention to just those problems which are involved on the witness stand. It is perhaps no exaggeration to say that a new special science has even grown up which deals exclusively with the reliability of memory. It started in Germany and has had there for some years even a magazine of its own. But many investigations in France and the United States tended from the start in the same direction, and the work spread rapidly over the psychological laboratories of the world. Rich material has been gathered, and yet practical jurisprudence is, on the whole, still unaware of it; and while the alienist is always a welcome guest in the court room, the psychologist is still a stranger there. The Court would rather listen for whole days to the "science" of the handwriting experts than allow a witness to be examined with regard to his memory and his power of perception, his attention and his associations, his volition and his suggestibility, with methods which are in accord with the exact work of experimental psychology. It is so much easier everywhere to be satisfied with sharp demarcation lines and to listen only to a yes or no; the man is sane or insane, and if he is sane, he speaks the truth or he lies. The psychologist would upset this satisfaction completely.

The administration of an oath is partly responsible for the

wrong valuation of the evidence. Its seriousness and solemnity suggest that the conditions for complete truth are given if the witness is ready not to lie. We are too easily inclined to confuse the idea of truth in a subjective and in an objective sense. A German proverb says, "Children and fools speak the truth," and with it goes the old "*In vino veritas.*" Of course, no one can suppose that children, fools, and tipsy men have a deeper insight into true relations than the sober and grown-up remainder of mankind. What is meant is only that all the motives are lacking which, in our social turmoil, may lead others to the intentional hiding of the truth. Children do not suppress the truth, because they are naïve; the fools do not suppress it, because they are reckless; and the mind under the influence of wine does not suppress it, because the suppressing mechanism of inhibition is temporarily paralysed by alcohol. The subjective truth may thus be secured, and yet the idle talk of the drunkard and the child and the fool may be objectively untrue from beginning to end. It is in this way only that the oath by its religious background and by its connection with threatened punishment can work for truth. It can and will remove to a high degree the intention to hide the truth, but it may be an open question to what degree it can increase the objective truthfulness.

Of course, everyone knows that the oath helps in at least one more direction in curbing misstatements. It not only suppresses the intentional lie, but it focusses the attention on the details of the statement. It excludes the careless, hasty, chance recollection, and stirs the deliberate attention of the witness. He feels the duty of putting his best will into the effort to reproduce the whole truth and nothing but the truth. No psychologist will deny this effect. He will ask only whether the intention alone is sufficient for success and whether the memory is really improved in every respect by increased attention. We are not always sure that our functions run best when we concentrate our effort on them and turn the full light of attention on the details. We may speak fluently, but the moment we begin to give attention to the special movements of our lips and of our tongue in speaking and make a special effort to produce the movements correctly, we are badly hampered. Is it so sure that our memory works faultlessly simply because we earnestly want it to behave well? We may try hard to think of a name and it will not appear in consciousness; and when we have thought of something else for a long time, the desired name suddenly slips into our mind. May it not be in a similar way that the effort for correct recollection under oath may prove powerless to a degree which public opinion underestimates? And no subjective feeling of certainty can be an objective criterion for the desired truth.

A few years ago a painful scene occurred in Berlin, in the University Seminary of Professor von Liszt, the famous criminologist. The Professor had spoken about a book. One of the older students suddenly shouts, "I wanted to throw light on the matter from the standpoint of Christian morality!" Another student throws in, "I cannot stand that!" The first starts up, exclaiming, "You have insulted me!" The second clenches his fist and cries, "If you say another word —" The first draws a revolver. The second rushes madly upon him. The Professor steps between them and, as he grasps the man's arm, the revolver goes off. General uproar. In that moment Professor Liszt secures order and asks a part of the students to write an exact account of all that has happened. The whole had been a comedy, carefully planned and rehearsed by the three actors for the purpose of studying the exactitude of observation and recollection. Those who did not write the report at once were, part of them, asked to write it the next day or a week later; and others had to depose their observations under cross-examination. The whole objective performance was cut up into fourteen little parts which referred partly to actions, partly to words. As mistakes there were counted the omissions, the wrong additions and the alterations. The smallest number of mistakes gave twenty-six per cent. of erroneous statements; the largest was eighty per cent. The reports with reference to the second half of the performance, which was more strongly emotional, gave an average of fifteen per cent. more mistakes than those of the first half. Words were put into the mouths of men who had been silent spectators during the whole short episode; actions were attributed to the chief participants of which not the slightest trace existed; and essential parts of the tragi-comedy were completely eliminated from the memory of a number of witnesses.

This dramatic psychological experiment of six years ago opened up a long series of similar tests in a variety of places, with a steady effort to improve the conditions. The most essential condition remained, of course, always the complete naïveté of the witnesses, as the slightest suspicion on their part would destroy the value of the experiment. It seems desirable even that the writing of the protocol should still be done in a state of belief. There was, for instance, two years ago in Göttingen a meeting of a scientific association, made up of jurists, psychologists, and physicians, all, therefore, men well trained in careful observation. Somewhere in the same street there was that evening a public festivity of the carnival. Suddenly, in the midst of the scholarly meeting, the doors open, a clown in highly coloured costume rushes in in mad excitement, and a negro with a revolver in hand follows him. In the middle of the hall first the one, then the other, shouts wild phrases; then the one falls to the ground, the other jumps on him;

then a shot, and suddenly both are out of the room. The whole affair took less than twenty seconds. All were completely taken by surprise, and no one, with the exception of the President, had the slightest idea that every word and action had been rehearsed beforehand, or that photographs had been taken of the scene. It seemed most natural that the President should beg the members to write down individually an exact report, inasmuch as he felt sure that the matter would come before the courts. Of the forty reports handed in, there was only one whose omissions were calculated as amounting to less than twenty per cent. of the characteristic acts; fourteen had twenty to forty per cent of the facts omitted; twelve omitted forty to fifty per cent., and thirteen still more than fifty per cent. But besides the omissions there were only six among the forty which did not contain positively wrong statements; in twenty-four papers up to ten per cent, of the statements were free inventions, and in ten answers — that is, in one-fourth of the papers, — more than ten per cent of the statements were absolutely false, in spite of the fact that they all came from scientifically trained observers. Only four persons, for instance, among forty noticed that the negro had nothing on his head; the others gave him a derby, or a high hat, and so on. In addition to this, a red suit, a brown one, a striped one, a coffee-coloured jacket, shirt sleeves, and similar costumes were invented for him. He wore in reality white trousers and a black jacket with a large red necktie. The scientific commission which reported the details of the inquiry came to the general statement that the majority of the observers omitted or falsified about half of the processes which occurred completely in their field of vision. As was to be expected, the judgment as to the time duration of the act varied between a few seconds and several minutes.

It is not necessary to tell more of these dramatic experiments, which have recently become the fashion and almost a sport, and which will still have to be continued with a great variety of conditions if the psychological laws involved are really to be cleared up. There are many points, for instance, in which the results seem still contradictory. In some cases it was shown that the mistakes made after a week were hardly more frequent more than those made after a day. Other experiments seemed to indicate that the number of mistakes steadily increases with the length of time which has elapsed. Again, some experiments suggest that the memory of the two sexes is not essentially different, while the majority of the tests seems to speak for very considerable difference. Experiments with school children, especially, seem to show that the girls have a better memory than the boys as far as omissions are concerned; they forget less. But they have a worse memory than the boys as far as correctness is concerned; they unintentionally falsify more.

We may consider here still another point which is more directly connected with our purpose. A well-known psychologist showed three pictures, rich in detail, but well adapted to the interest of children, to a large number of boys and girls. They looked at each picture for fifteen seconds and then wrote a full report of everything they could remember. After that they were asked to underline those parts of their reports of which they felt so absolutely certain that they would be ready to take an oath before court on the underlined words. The young people put forth their best efforts, and yet the results showed that there were almost as many mistakes in the underlined sentences as in the rest. This experiment has been often repeated and the results make clear that this happens in a smaller and yet still surprising degree in the case of adults also. The grown-up students of my laboratory commit this kind of perjury all the time.

Subtler experiments which were carried on in my laboratory for a long time showed that this subjective feeling of certainty can not only obtain in different degrees, but has, with different individuals, quite different mental structure and meaning. We found that there were, above all, two distinct classes. For one of those types certainty in the recollection of an experience would rest very largely upon the vividness of the image. For the other type it would depend upon the congruity of an image with other previously accepted images; that is, on the absence of conflicts, when the experience judged about is imagined as part of a wide setting of past experiences. But the most surprising result of those studies was perhaps that the feeling of certainty stands in no definite relation to the attention with which the objects are observed. If we turn our attention with strongest effort to certain parts of a complex impression, we may yet feel in our recollection more certain about those parts of which we hardly took notice than about those to which we devoted our attention. The correlations between attention, recollection, and feeling of certainty become the more complex the more we carefully study them. Not only the self-made psychology of the average juryman, but also the scanty psychological statements which judge and attorney find in the large compendiums on Evidence fall to pieces if a careful examination approaches the mental facts.

The sources of error begin, of course, before the recollection sets in. The observation itself may be defective and illusory; wrong associations may make it imperfect; judgments may misinterpret the experience; and suggestive influences may falsify the data of the senses. Everyone knows the almost unlimited individual differences in the power of correct observation and judgment. Everyone knows that there are persons who, under favourable conditions, see what they are expected to see. The prestidigitateurs, the fakirs, the spiritualists could not play their tricks if they could not rely on associations and suggestions, and it would not be so difficult to read proofs if we did not usually see the letters which we expect. But we can abstract here from the distortions which enter into the perception itself; we have discussed them before. The mistakes of recollection alone are now the object of our inquiry and we may throw light on them from still another side.

Many of us remember minutes in which we passed through an experience with a distinct and almost uncanny feeling of having passed through it once before. The words which we hear, the actions which we see, we remember exactly that we experienced them a long time ago. The case is rare with men, but with women extremely frequent, and there are few women who do not know the state. An idea is there distinctly coupled with the feeling of remembrance and recognition, and yet it is only an associated sensation, resulting from fatigue or excitement, and without the slightest objective basis in the past. The psychologist feels no difficulty in explaining it, but it ought to stand as a great warning signal before the minds of those who believe that the feeling of certainty in recollection secures objective truth. There is no new principle involved, of course, when the ideas which stream into consciousness spring from one's own imagination instead of being produced by the outer impressions of our surroundings. Any imaginative thought may slip into our consciousness and may carry with it in the same way that curious feeling that it is merely the repetition of something we have experienced before.

A striking illustration is well known to those who have ever taken the trouble to approach the depressing literature of modern mysticism. There we find an abundance of cases reported which seem to prove that either prophetic fortune tellers or inspired dreams have anticipated the real future of a man's life with the subtlest details and with the most uncanny foresight. But as soon as we examine these wonderful stories, we find that the coincidences are surprising only in those cases in which the dreams and the prophecies have been written down after the realisation. Whenever the visions were given to the protocol before-hand, the percentage of true realisations remains completely within the narrow limits of chance coincidents and natural probability. In other words, there cannot be any doubt that the reports of such prophecies which are communicated after having been realised are falsified. That does not reflect in the least on the subjective veracity; our satisfied client of the clever fortune teller would feel ready to take oath to his illusions of memory; but illusions they remain. He also, in most cases, feels sure that he told the dream to the whole family the next morning exactly as it happened; only when it is possible to call the members of the family to a scientific witness stand, does it become evident that the essentials of the dream varied in all directions from the real later occurrence. The real present occurrence completely transforms the reminiscences of the past prophecy and every happening is apperceived with the illusory overtone of having been foreseen.

We must always keep in mind that a content of consciousness is in itself independent of its relation to the past and has thus in itself no mark which can indicate whether it was experienced once before or not. The feeling of belonging to our past life may associate itself thus just as well with a perfectly new idea of our imagination as with a real reproduction of an earlier state of mind. As a matter of course, the opposite can thus happen, too; that is, an earlier experience may come to our memory stripped of every reference to the past, standing before our mind like a completely new product of imagination. To point again to an apparently mysterious experience: the crystal gazer feels in his half hypnotic state a free play of inspired imagination, and yet in reality he experiences only a stirring up of the deeper layers of memory pictures. They rush to his mind without any reference to their past origin, picturing a timeless truth which is surprisingly correct only because it is the result of a sharpened memory. Yes, we fill the blanks of our perceptions constantly with bits of reproduced memory material and take those reproductions for immediate impressions. In short, we never know from the material itself whether we remember, perceive, or imagine, and in the borderland regions there must result plenty of confusion which cannot always remain without dangerous consequences in the court-room.

Still another phenomenon is fairly familiar to everyone, and only the courts have not yet discovered it. There are different types of memory, which in a very crude and superficial classification might be grouped as visual, acoustical, and motor types. There are persons who can reproduce a landscape or a painting in full vivid colours and with sharp outlines throughout the field, while they would be unable to hear internally a melody or the sound of a voice. There are others with whom every tune can easily resound in recollection and who can hardly read a letter of a friend without hearing his voice in every word, while they are utterly unable to awake an optical image. There are others again whose sensorial reproduction is poor in both respects; they feel intentions of movement, as of speaking, of writing, of acting, whenever they reconstruct past experience. In reality the number of types is much larger. Scores of memory variations can be discriminated. Let your friends describe how they have before their minds yesterday's dinner table and the conversation around it, and there will not be two whose memory shows the same scheme and method. Now we should not ask a short-sighted man for the slight visual details of a far distant scene, yet it cannot be safer to ask a man of the acoustical memory type for strictly optical recollections. No one on the witness stand is to-day examined to ascertain in what directions his memory is probably trustworthy and reliable; he may be asked what he has seen, what he has heard, what he has spoken, how he has acted, and yet even a most superficial test might show that the mechanism of his memory would be excellent for one of these four groups of questions and utterly useless for the others, however solemnly he might keep his oath.

The courts will have to learn, sooner or later, that the individual differences of men can be tested to-day by the methods of experimental psychology far beyond anything which common sense and social experience suggest. Modern law welcomes, for instance, for identification of criminals all the discoveries of anatomists and physiologists as to the individual differences; even the different play of lines in the thumb is carefully registered in wax. But no one asks for the striking differences as to those mental details which the psychological experiments on memory and attention, on feeling and imagination, on perception and discrimination, on judgment and suggestion, on emotion and volition, have brought out in the last decade. Other sciences are less slow to learn. It has been found, for instance, that the psychological speech impulse has for every individual a special character as to intonation and melody. At once the philologists came and made the most brilliant use of this psychological discovery. They have taken, for instance, whole epic texts and examined those lines as to which it was doubtful whether they belonged originally to the poem or were later interpolations.

Wherever the speech intonation agreed with that of the whole song, they acknowledged the authentic origin, and where it did not agree they recognised an interpolation of the text. Yet the lawyers might learn endlessly more from the psychologists about individual differences than the philologians have done. They must only understand that the working of the mental mechanism in a personality depends on the constant coöperation of simple and elementary functions which the modern laboratory experiment can isolate and test. If those simplest elements are understood, their complex combination becomes necessary; just as the whole of a geometrical curve becomes necessary as soon as its analytical formula is understood for the smallest part.

But the psychological assistance ought not to be confined to the discrimination of memory types and other individual differences. The experimentalist cannot forget how abundant are the new facts of memory variations which have come out of experiments on attention and inhibition. We know and can test with the subtlest means the waves of fluctuating attention through which ideas become reinforced and weakened. We know, above all, the inhibitory influences which result from excitements and emotions which may completely change the products of an otherwise faithful memory.

A concrete illustration may indicate the method of the experimenters. The judge has to make up his mind as soon as there is any doubt on which side the evidence on an issue of fact preponderates. If it can be presupposed that both sides intend to speak the truth he is ready to consider that the one side had, perhaps, a more frequent opportunity to watch the facts in question, the other side, perhaps, saw them more recently; the one saw them, perhaps, under especially impressive circumstances, the other, perhaps, with further knowledge of the whole situation, and so on. Of course, his buckram-bound volumes of old decisions guide him, but those decisions report again only that the one or the other judge, relying on his common-sense, thought recency more weighty than frequency, or frequency more important than impressiveness, or perhaps the opposite. It is the same way in which common-sense tells a man what kind of diet is most nourishing. Yet what responsible physician would ignore the painstaking experiments of the physiological laboratory, determining exactly the quantitative results as to the nourishing value of eggs or milk or meat or bread? The judges ignore the fact that with the same accuracy their common-sense can be transformed into careful measurements the results of which may widely differ from haphazard opinion. The psychologist, of course, has to reduce the complex facts to simple principles and elements. An investigation, devoted to this problem of the relative effectiveness of recency, frequency, and vividness was carried on in my psychological laboratory. Here we used simple pairs of coloured papers and printed figures, or colours and words, or words and figures, or colours and forms, and so on. A series of ten such pairs may be exposed successively in a lighted field, each time one colour and one figure of two digits. But one pair, perhaps the third, is repeated as the seventh, and thus impresses itself by its frequency; another pair, perhaps the fifth, comes with impressive vividness, from the fact that instead of two digits, suddenly three are used. The last pair has, of course, the advantage in that it sticks to the mind from its position at the end; it remains the most recent, which is not inhibited by any following pair. After a pause the colours are shown again and every one of the subjects has to write down the figures together with which he believes himself to have seen the particular colours. Is the vivid pair, or the frequently repeated pair, or the recent pair better remembered? Of course, the experiment was made under most different conditions, with different pauses, different material, different length of the series, different influences, different distribution, different subjects, but after some years of work, facts showed themselves which can stand as facts. The relative value of the various conditions for exact recollection became really measurable. They may and must be corrected by further experiments, but they are raised from the first above the level of the chance opinions of the lawyer-psychologist.

All this remains entirely within the limits of the normal healthy individuality. Nothing of all that we have mentioned belongs to the domain of the physician. Where the alienist has to speak, that is, where pathological amnesia destroys the memory of the witness, or where hallucinations of disease, or fixed ideas deprive the witness's remembrance of their value, there the psychologist is not needed. It is in normal mental life and its border-land regions that the progress of psychological science cannot be further ignored. No railroad or ship company would appoint to a responsible post in its service men whose eyesight had not been tested for colour blindness. There may be only one among thirty or forty who cannot distinguish at a distance the red from the green lantern. Yet if he slips into the service without being tested, his slight defect, which does not disturb him in practical life and which he may never have noticed if he was not just picking red strawberries among green leaves, may be sufficient to bring about the most disastrous wrecking of two trains or the most horrible collision of steamers. In the life of justice trains are wrecked and ships are colliding too often, simply because the law does not care to examine the mental colour blindness of the witness's memory.

And yet we have not even touched one factor which, more than anything else, devastates memory and plays havoc with our best intended recollections: that is, the power of suggestion.

4

The Detection of Crime

As old as the history of crime is the history of cruelties exercised, in the service of justice, for the discovery of criminal facts. Man has the power to hide his knowledge and his memories by silence and by lies, and the infliction of physical and mental pain has always seemed the quickest way to untie the tongue and to force the confession of truth. Through thousands of years, in every land on the globe, accomplices have been named, crimes have been acknowledged, secrets have been given up, under threats and tortures which overwhelmed the will to resist. The imagination of the Orient invented more dastardly tortures than that of the Occident; the mediaeval Inquisition brought the system to perhaps fuller perfection than later centuries; and to-day the fortresses of Russia are said to witness tortures which would be impossible in non-Slavic lands. And, although the forms have changed, can there be any doubt that even in the United States brutality is still a favourite method of undermining the mental resistance of the accused? There are no longer any thumb-screws, but the lower orders of the police have still uncounted means to make the prisoner's life uncomfortable and perhaps intolerable, and to break down his energy. A rat put secretly into a woman's cell may exhaust her nervous system and her inner strength till she is unable to stick to her story. The dazzling light and the cold-water hose and the secret blow seem still to serve, even if nine-tenths of the newspaper stories of the "third degree" are exaggerated.

Worst of all are the brutal shocks given with fiendish cruelty to the terrified imagination of the suspect.

Decent public opinion stands firmly against such barbarism; and this opposition springs not only from sentimental horror and from aesthetic disgust: stronger, perhaps, than either of these is the instinctive conviction that the method is ineffective in bringing out the real truth. At all times, innocent men have been accused by the tortured ones, crimes which were never committed have been confessed, infamous lies have been invented, to satisfy the demands of the torturers. Under pain and fear a man may make any admission which will relieve his suffering, and, still more misleading, his mind may lose the power to discriminate between illusion and real memory. Enlightened juries have begun to understand how the ends of justice are frustrated by such methods. Only recently an American jury, according to the newspapers, acquitted a suspect who, after a previous denial, confessed with full detail to having murdered a girl whose slain body had been found. The detectives had taken the shabby young man to the undertaking-rooms, led him to the side of the coffin, suddenly whipped back the sheet, exposing the white bruised face, and abruptly demanded, "When did you see her?" He sank on his knees and put his hands over his face; but they dragged him to his feet and ordered him to place his right hand on the forehead of the body. Shuddering, he obeyed, and the next moment again collapsed. The detectives pulled him again to his feet, and fired at him question after question, forcing him to stroke the girl's hair and cheeks; and, evidently without control of his mind, he affirmed all that his torturers asked, and, in his half-demented state, even added details to his untrue story.

The clean conscience of a modern nation rejects every such brutal scheme in the search of truth, and yet is painfully aware that the accredited means for unveiling the facts are too often insufficient. The more complex the machinery of our social life, the easier it seems to cover the traces of crime and to hide the outrage by lies and deception. Under these circumstances, it is surprising and seems unjustifiable that lawyers and laymen alike should not have given any attention, so far, to the methods of measurement of association which experimental psychology has developed in recent years. Of course, the same holds true of many other methods of the psychological laboratory — methods in the study of memory and attention, feeling and will, perception and judgment, suggestion and emotion. In every one of these fields the psychological experiment could be made helpful to the purposes of court and law. But it is the study and measurement of associations which have particular value in those realms where the barbarisms of the third degree were formerly in use. The chronoscope of the modern psychologist has become, and will become more and more, for the student of crime what the microscope is for the student of disease. It makes visible that which remains otherwise invisible, and shows minute facts which allow a clear diagnosis. The physician needs his magnifier to find out whether there are tubercles in the sputum: the legal psychologist may in the future use his mental microscope to make sure whether there are lies in the mind of the suspect.

The study of the association of ideas has attracted the students of the human mind since the day of Aristotle; but only in the last century have we come to inquire systematically into the laws and causes of these mental connections. Of course, every one knows that our memory ideas link themselves with our impressions — that a face reminds us of a name, or a name of a face; that one word calls another to mind; that even smell or taste may wake in us manifold associations. But out of such commonplaces grew a whole systematic science, and the school of associationists began to explain our entire mental life as essentially the interplay of such associations. There are the outer associations of time and place, where one thing reminds us of another together with which we experienced it. There are inner associations, where one thing awakens in our minds something else which has similarity to it, or to which it is related as a part to the whole or the whole to a part, and so on. The word "dog" may call up in my mind, perhaps, the memory-picture of a particular dog, or the name of that dog, or the idea of a house in which I saw it; or it may bring up the superordinated idea, "animal," or the subordinated, "terrier," or the coördinated, "cat," or the part, "tail"; or perhaps it may suggest to me the German translation for dog, or a painting with dogs in it: there are no end of possibilities. But the psychologists were not satisfied with grouping the various cases; their chief aim was to determine the conditions under which they arise, the influence which the frequency or the recency or the vividness or the combination of special experiences has on the choice of the resulting idea.

In the last few decades, then, has arisen the new science, experimental psychology, which, like physics and chemistry, has its own workshops, wherein mental facts are brought under experimental test in the same way as in the natural sciences. With the application of experimental methods, the study of association took at once a new turn. In the laboratory we are not confined to the chance material which daily life offers; we can prepare and control the situation. For instance, I may use a list of one hundred substantives, and read one after the other to my subject, and ask him to give me the first word which enters his mind. I receive thus one hundred associations which are independent of any intentional selection, showing just the paths of least resistance in the mind of my man. I may use them, for instance, to make statistics as to their character: if the outer associations prevail, I have a type of mind before me other than in the case of a preponderance of inner associations; if the superordinations prevail, I have an intellect other than if the subordinations were in the majority. Or I may study the influences of preceding impressions. Perhaps I read to my man a story or showed him some pictures before I gave him the one hundred words for association; the effect of that recent experience will show itself at once. In this way the variations are endless.

But one aspect dominates in importance: I can measure the time of this connection of ideas. Suppose that both my subject and I have little electrical instruments between the lips, which, by the least movement of speaking, make or break an electric current passing through an electric clockwork whose index moves around a dial ten times in every second. One revolution of the index thus means the tenth part of a second, and, as the whole dial is divided into one hundred parts, every division indicates the thousandth part of a second. My index stands quietly till I move my lips to make, for instance, the word "dog." In that moment the electric current causes the pointer to revolve. My subject, as soon as he hears the word, is to speak out as quickly as possible the first association which comes to his mind. He perhaps shouts out "cat," and the movement of his lips breaks the current, stops the pointer, and thus allows me to read from the clockwork in thousandth parts of a second the time which passed between my speaking the word and his naming the association. Of course, this time includes not only the time for the process of association, but also the time for the hearing of the word, for the understanding, for the impulse of speaking, and so on. But all these smaller periods I can easily determine. I may find out how long it takes if my subject does not associate anything, but simply repeats the word I give him. If the mere repetition of the word "dog" takes him 325 thousandths of a second, while the bringing up of the word "cat" took 975 thousandths, I conclude that the difference of 650 thousandths was necessary for the process of associating "cat" and "dog."

In this way, during the last twenty years, there has developed an exact and subtle study of mental associations, and through such very careful observation of the time-differences between associations a deep insight has been won into the whole mental mechanism. The slightest changes of our psychical connections can be discovered and traced by these slight variations of time, which are, of course, entirely unnoticeable so long as no exact measurements are introduced. The last few years have finally brought the latest step: the theoretical studies have been made useful to practical life. Like many other branches of experimental psychology, the doctrine of association has become adjusted to the practical problems of education, of medicine, of art, of commerce, and of law. It is the last which chiefly concerns us here — a kind of investigation which began in Germany and has since been developed here and abroad.

For instance, our purpose may be to find out whether a suspected person has really participated in a certain crime. He declares that he is innocent, that he was not present when the outrage occurred, and that he is not even familiar with the locality. An innocent man will not object to our proposing a series of one hundred associations to demonstrate his innocence. A guilty man, of course, will not object, either, as a declination would indicate a fear of betraying himself; he cannot refuse, and yet affirm his innocence. Moreover, he will feel sure that no questions can bring out any facts which he wants to keep hidden in his soul; he will be on the lookout. As long as nothing more is demanded than that he speak the first word which comes to his mind, when another word is spoken to him, there is indeed no legal and no practical reason for declining, as long as innocence is professed. Such an experiment will at once become interesting in three different directions as soon as we mix into our list of one hundred words a number, perhaps thirty, which stand in more or less close connection to the crime in question — words which refer to the details of the locality, or to the persons present at the crime, or to the probable motive, or to the professed alibi, and so on. The first direction of our interest is toward the choice of the associations. Of course, every one believes that he would be sure to admit only harmless words to his lips; but the conditions of the experiment quickly destroy that feeling of safety. As soon as a dangerous association rushes to the consciousness, it tries to push its way out. It may, indeed, need some skill to discover the psychical influence, as the suspected person may have self-control enough not to give away the dangerous idea directly; but the suppressed idea remains in consciousness, and taints the next association, or perhaps the next but one, without his knowledge.

He has, perhaps, slain a woman in her room, and yet protests that he has never been in her house. By the side of her body was a cage with a canary-bird. I therefore mix into my list of words also "bird." His mind is full of the gruesome memory of his heinous deed. The word "bird," therefore, at once awakens the association "canary-bird" in his consciousness; yet he is immediately aware that this would be suspicious, and he succeeds, before the dangerous word comes to his lips, in substituting the harmless word "sparrow." Yet my next word, or perhaps my second or third next, is "colour," and his prompt association is "yellow": the canary-bird is still in his mind, and shows its betraying influence. The preparation of the list of words to be called thus needs psychological judgment and insight if a man with quick self-control is to be trapped. In most cases, however, there is hardly any need of relying on the next and following words, as the primary associations for the critical words unveil themselves for important evidence directly enough.

Yet not only the first associations are interesting. There is interest in another direction in the associations which result from a second and a third repetition of the series. Perhaps after half an hour, I go once more through the whole list. The subject gives once more his hundred replies. An analysis of the results will show that most of the words which he now gives are the same which he gave the first time; pronouncing the words has merely accentuated his tendency to associate them in the same connection as before. If it was "house" — "window" first, then it will probably be "house"—"window" again. But a number of associations have been changed, and a careful analysis will show that these are first of all the suspicious ones. Those words which by their connection with the crime stir up deep emotional complexes of ideas will throw ever new associations into consciousness, while the indifferent ones will link themselves in a superficial way without change. To a certain degree, this variation of the dangerous associations is reinforced by the intentional effort of the suspected. He does not feel satisfied with his first words, and hopes that other words may better hide his real thoughts, not knowing that just this change is to betray him.

But most important is the third direction of inquiry: more

characteristic than the choice and the constancy of the associations is their involuntary retardation by emotional influence. A word which stirs emotional memories will show an association-time twice or three times as long as a commonplace idea. It may be said at once that it is not ordinarily necessary, even for legal purposes, that the described measurement be in thousandths of a second; the differences of time which betray a bad conscience or a guilty knowledge of certain facts are large enough to be easily measured in hundredths or even in tenths of a second; though measurements for the theoretical purposes of psychology require, indeed, a division of the second into a thousand parts. In the following legal division I shall, therefore, refer to differences in tenths of a second only.

The absolute time of associations is, of course, quite different for different persons; to link familiar ideas like "chair" — "table" or "black" — "white" may take for the slow type more than a full second, while the alert mind may not need more than half a second. Thus we begin by finding the average for each individual, and all our interest goes into the deviations from this average. That a certain association should take one and a half seconds would be a very suspicious retardation for the quick mind which normally associates in three quarters, while it would be quite normal for the slow thinker. And here, again, it may be mentioned that the retardation is not always confined to the dangerous association alone, but often comes in a still more pregnant way in the following or the next following association, which on the surface looks entirely harmless. The emotional shock has perturbed the working of the mechanism, and the path for all associations is blocked. The analysis of these secondary time-retardations is the factor which demands the greatest psychological skill. A few illustrations from practical life may make the whole method clearer.

An educated young man of eighteen lived in the house of an uncle. The old gentleman went to consult a nerve specialist in regard to some slight nervous trouble of the younger friend. On that occasion he confided his recent suspicion that the young man might be a thief. Money had repeatedly been taken from a drawer and from a trunk; until lately he had had suspicions only of the servants; he had notified the police, and detectives had watched them. He was most anxious to find out whether his new suspicion was true, as he wanted, in that case, to keep the matter out of court, in the interest of the family. The physician, Dr. Jung, in Zurich, arranged that the young man come for an examination of his nerves. He then proposed to him a list of a hundred associations as part of the medical inspection. The physician said "head," the patient associated "nose"; then "green" — "blue," "water" — "air," "long" — "short," "five" — "six," "wool" — "cloth," and so on, the average time of these commonplace connections being 1.6 seconds. But there were thirty-seven dangerous words scattered among the hundred — words that had to do with the things in the room from which the money was abstracted, or with the theft and its punishment, or with some possible motives. There appeared, for instance, the word "thief." The association "burglar" seemed quite natural, but it took the boy suddenly 4.6 seconds to reach it. In the same way "police" — " theft" took 3.6 seconds, "jail" — "penitentiary" 4.2 seconds. In other cases the dangerous word itself came with normal automatic quickness, but the emotional disturbance became evident in the retardation of the next word. For instance, "key" — "false key" took only 1.6 seconds, but the following trivial association "stupid"—"clever" grew to 3.0 seconds. "Crime" — "theft" came again promptly in 1.8, but the inner shock was so strong that the commonplace word "cook" was entirely inhibited and did not produce an association at all in 20 seconds. In the same way "bread" — "water" rushed forward in 1.6 seconds, but this characteristic choice, the supposed diet of the jail, stopped the associative mechanism again for the following trivial word. It would lead too far to go further into the analysis of the case, but it may be added that a repetition of the same series showed the characteristic variations in the region of the suspicious words. While "crime" had brought "theft" the first time, it was the second time replaced by "murder"; "discover" brought the first time "wrong," the second time "grasp." In the harmless words there was hardly any change at all. But, finally, a subtle analysis of the selection of words and of the retardations pointed to sufficient details to make a clear diagnosis. The physician told the young man that he had stolen; the boy protested vehemently. Then the physician gave him the subtle points unveiled by the associations — how he had bought a watch with the money and had given presents to his sister; and the boy confessed everything, and was saved from jail by the early discovery. The brutalities of the third degree would hardly have yielded such a complete result, nor the technicalities of legal evidence, either.

Of course, this case is that of a highly sensitive mind with the strong feelings of a bad conscience. A professional tough criminal would not show such intense emotions, and hence not such long retardations, if he were as unsuspicious and unaware of the purposes of the experiment as that boy was. But what would be the situation of such a trained criminal who had no conscience and who knew beforehand that the experiment was to determine whether or not he lied or spoke the truth?

In that case, another group of facts is to be considered. We might expect from such a subject very little lengthening of the simple association-time by emotion, but instead of it a considerable lengthening by conscious effort to avoid suspicious and dangerous associations, provided that he were anxious to hide the damaging truth. As soon as a critical word were offered, he would be on the look-out not to betray the first word which came over the threshold of consciousness, but to make sure first that it was harmless, and to replace it if it were dangerous. Experiment shows that such watching and conscious sanctioning takes time, and the replacing of the unfit word by a fitting word brings still larger loss of time; nobody is able to look out for the harmlessness of his associations and yet to associate them with the average quickness with which the commonplace ideas are brought forth. If the dangerous words show association-times of unusual shortness, it is necessary to suppose that the subject of the experiment makes no effort to suppress the truth; the short time proves that he lets the ideas go as they will, without his sifting, sanctioning, and retouching. Even the best bluffer will thus be trapped in his effort to conceal anything, by time-differences which he himself cannot notice.

As an illustration of a case of such a type, I may speak of experiments that I carried on recently for several days in a Western penitentiary with a self-confessed multi-murderer. He played the star witness in a trial against a man whom his confession accused as an accomplice. It made hardly a difference whether the view of the prosecution or the view of the defence was taken: seen from any side, the witness offered a psychological problem of unusual interest. And its importance did not decrease when it was found out, through the verdict of the jury, that the defendant was innocent and had no connection with the crimes of the witness. No side doubted at any time that this was one of the most persistent murderers of modern time, and no side could deny that he was, during the trial, an imperturbable witness with the mildest manners, with quiet serenity, and with the appearance of a man who has found his peace in God.

The first problem for the psychologist was whether the confession of the witness was a chain of conscious lies or whether he himself really believed what he told the court. No outer evidence was fit to settle this question of his mental attitude, and it seemed thus interesting to study whether it might be possible to decide it by the association method.

I had the good chance to see the murderer at once on the witness stand. As my seat was at the small table of the attorneys for the prosecution, I had him only a few feet from me for careful observation. I cannot deny that my impression on that first morning was very unfavourable. His profile, especially the jaw, appeared to me most brutal and vulgar; I also saw at once the deformation of the ear, the irregularity in the movements of the eyes, and the abnormal lower lip. That this was the profile of a murderer seemed to me not improbable, but that this man had become a sincere religious convert seemed to me quite incredible. Yet, I did not consult my antipathies; I had to rely on my experiments, which I started the following day. This is, of course, not the place to set down a scientific report of the nearly one hundred groups of tests and experiments which were completed; they belong in scholarly archives. Most of them referred to the memory, the attention, the feelings, the will, the judgment, and the suggestibility. Our interest here belongs only to the association experiments and to some related tests. Thus the report here covers only a small section of the case, and ignores entirely everything which does not refer to the subjective veracity.

I told the witness directly that I had come to examine his mind and find out what was really at the bottom of his heart. He at once declared himself perfectly ready to undergo any test. If he thought that he, the experienced poker-player, could easily hide his inmost mind and could deceive me with cant and lies, I turned the tables on him quickly. I began with some simple psychological tricks with which every student of psychology is familiar, but which were naturally unknown and somewhat uncanny to the witness. For instance, I covered one of his eyes and asked him to fixate with the other eye a little cross on the table, and to watch at the same time a cent piece which I moved at the side of the cross. Suddenly I told him that he would not see the cent any more — indeed, it had disappeared; and as he did not know that we all have a blind spot at the entrance-place of the optical nerve in the retina, he was much struck by my foreknowledge of such a defect in his eye. Or, I showed him the drawing of a stair which he saw as such; observing his eye movements, I told him that he now did not see the stair any more, but an overhanging wall, and again he was astonished at my knowing everything in his soul. In a similar way, I used some tactual illusions, and soon he was entirely under the spell of the belief that I had some special scientific powers.

Then I began with a real experiment. I told him that I should call at first fifty words, and each time, when he heard a word, he was to name to me as quickly as possible the first thing which came to his mind on the hearing of the word. I asked him not to choose the words intentionally, but to let them go without any reflection; I added that I should learn all from the ideas which he would bring up. My first word was "river," he associated "water"; then "ox," he said "yoke"; "mountain," he said "hill"; "tobacco," he said "pipe." All the interest thus seemed to belong to the choice of the words, and he saw that I wrote his answers down. But the fact is that I did something else also; I measured in fractions of a second the time between my calling the word and his giving a reply. Between his hearing of the word "river" and his speaking the word "water," eight-tenths of a second passed; between "ox" — "yoke," six-tenths; between "tobacco" — "pipe," eight-tenths. On the whole, seven to eight-tenths of a second was the very short standard time for those associations which represented familiar ideas.

Now, there were mixed in among the fifty words many which had direct relation to his criminal career and to his professed religious conversion — for instance, the words confession, revolver, religion, heaven, jury, death, Bible, pardon, railroad, blood, jail, prayer, and some names of his victims and of his alleged accomplices. Let us not forget that he was fully under the belief that I had a special power to discover from his spoken words the real tendencies of his mind. If he had had anything to hide, he would have been constantly on the lookout that no treacherous word should slip in. If a word like "confession" or something similar were called among harmless ones, he would never shout at once the first word which came to his mind, but would have watched that no dangerous secret, perhaps "confession" — "humbug," came out and betrayed him. He would have quickly suppressed the word before it was spoken — and yet, however quickly he might have done it, it would have taken at least one or two seconds more; and he would have used the longer time the more freely, as he had no reason to suspect that time played any part in the experiment.

But the results show the very remarkable fact that the dangerous words brought, on the whole, no retardation of the associative process. After "tobacco"—"pipe" came with the same promptness "confession" —"truth," again in eight-tenths of a second, a time entirely insufficient for any inner deliberation or sanction or choice or correction: it is a time which just allows the speaking of the first idea which arises in the mind. "Heaven" — "God" took, again, less than a second, and so "religion" — "truth," "blood" — "knife," "governor" — "executive," "witness" — "stand," "minister" — "pulpit," "mine-owner" — "mine"; only "pardon" — "peace," "death" — "end," and similar more abstract words took about one and a half seconds, a time which is still too short for real inhibition and second thought. Even the names of his accomplices and of his victims awoke associations in less than nine-tenths of a second. The fact that these associations were produced by the witness in the minimum time, which made deliberation impossible, while he was convinced that the words would unveil his real mind, is strong evidence indeed that this man did not want consciously to hide anything, and that he himself really believed his confession.

If these experiments had been made with him before his confession, he would have stumbled over every third word, and many of his associations would have taken three seconds or more. He would have been unable, in spite of best efforts, to overcome the fear of betraying himself, and this fear would have retarded the associations in a way which would have trapped him unmistakably. But not only the short time, the choice of the associations also indicated clearly that, in an almost incredible manner, a mild, indifferent serenity had taken hold of his mind, and that his criminal life was of no concern to him any more. I gave him, for instance, the name of a city in which, according to his confession, he had been last to poison a victim and to dynamite his house; but in his mind the place did not connect itself any more with murder; in less than a second his mind joined it with "ocean."

It is evident from the association-times that no real emotion accompanied any of his memories of crime. He did not have and did not simulate a bad conscience. The emotional retardation of suspicious associations, characteristic of the average criminal, was, as expected, entirely lacking in this wholesale murderer. That does not mean that he lacks feeling; my experiments showed the opposite. To be sure, his sensitiveness for pain was, as with most criminals, much below the average. A deep pin-prick did not produce any reaction, and his whole touch sense was obtuse, while his eyes and ears were very sharp. But, in spite of this lack of organic pain, — he has never been ill, — he is sensitive to the immediate perception of suffering in others. Simulation is excluded: I measured the involuntary reactions. He really shivers at the thought of hurting others. I have no reason for doubting that he had this mental sensitiveness always; and that is no contradiction to the fact that he was spreading pain all around. Nearly all his crimes were performed in an impersonal way; he did not see the victims. He manufactured infernal machines, laid dynamite in the mines and bombs under gates, and thought of the suffering of the victims as little as the manufacturer of children's toys may think of the happiness of the little ones. He assured me that in those fifteen years of heinous deeds he never struck any one personally with his fist; that would have gone against his nerves. He exhibited tender feeling in all directions; he selected, for instance, very delicate colour combinations as those which he liked best among many which I showed him. His favourite colour seemed to be dark blue; any showy or loud dressing is disagreeable to him. He asserts, even, that he rarely drank any strong drinks: one glass of beer made him sleepy.

Yet his emotional life is simply dead — the small figures of his association-times would otherwise be quite impossible. And it may be added that even if his religious conversion is genuine, his so-called religion lacks also every sound and deep feeling; it is thoroughly utilitarian; he serves God because he will reward him after death.

The association experiments thus completely fulfilled their purpose: they gave a definite reply to a definite question which could hardly be answered by other methods of evidence. The association experiments proved that the murderer did not try to hide anything. Of course, this was only the first problem to be solved in the case. From this state of subjective truthfulness which interests the psychologist to the proof of objective truth which interests the court is still a very long way. It would have been possible, for instance, that all this was pseudo-religious auto-suggestion, or that it was a systematic illusion brought forth by the suggestions of detectives and lawyers, or that the witness was hypnotised, or that his mind was diseased. The experimental inquiry had to study all those and other possibilities; they formed the chief part of my experiments, but they do not belong here, as they have no relation to the method of association-measurement, which was the only concern of this discussion.

Of course, the theoretical importance of the method is independent of the practical importance of the cases in which it is applied. Multi-murderers are rare; but the simplest case of wrong-doing may demonstrate the success of the method just as well. No sharper contrast could be possible than that between the brutal criminal with his dynamite bombs and the lovely little girl with her chocolate bonbons whom I had seen a short time before. She was anemic and neurasthenic, and could not concentrate her attention on her work for her college examinations. She came to me for psychological advice. I asked her many questions as to her habits of life. Among other things, she assured me that she took wholesome and plentiful meals and was not allowed to buy sweets. Then I began some psychological experiments, and, among other tests, I started, at first rather aimlessly, with trivial associations. Her average association-time was slow, nearly 2 seconds. Very soon the word "money" brought the answer "candy," and it came with the quickness of 1.4 seconds. There was nothing remarkable in this. But the next word, "apron," harmless in itself, was 6 seconds in finding its association, and, furthermore, the association which resulted was "apron" — " chocolate." Both the retardation and the inappropriateness of this indicated that the foregoing pair had left an emotional shock, and the choice of the word "chocolate" showed that the disturbance resulted from the intrusion of the word "candy." The word "apron" had evidently no power at all compared with those associations which were produced by the candy-emotion.

I took this as a clue, and after twenty indifferent words which slowly restored her calmness of mind, I returned to the problem of sweets. Of course, she was now warned, and was evidently on the lookout. The result was that when I threw in the word "candy" again, she needed 4.5 seconds, and the outcome was the naïve association "never." This "never" was the first association that was neither substantive nor adjective. All the words before had evidently meant for her simply objects; but "candy" seemed to appeal to her as a hint, a question, a reproach, which she wanted to repudiate. She was clearly not aware that this mental change from a descriptive to a replying attitude was very suspicious; she must even have felt quite satisfied with her reply, for the next associations were short and to the point. After a while I began on the same line again. The unsuspicious word "box" brought quickly the equally unsuspicious "white"; and yet I knew at once that it was a candy-box, for the next word, "pound," brought the association "two" and the following, "book," after several seconds the unfit association "sweet." She was again not aware that she had betrayed the path of her imagination. In the course of three hundred associations I varied the subject repeatedly, and she remained to the end unconscious that she had given me all the information needed. Her surprise seemed still greater than her feeling of shame when I told her that she skipped her luncheons daily and had hardly any regular meals, but consumed every day several pounds of candy. With tears she made finally a full "confession." She had kept her injudicious diet a secret, as she had promised her parents not to spend any money for chocolate. The right diagnosis led me to make the right suggestions, and after a few weeks her health and strength were restored.

This trivial case with its foolish offence shows how psychological detective work may also be useful outside of the sphere of law. It not seldom becomes the serious interest of the educator and the physician to disentangle hidden thoughts, and the "third degree" of the school and of the consultation-room might easily be replaced by association experiments. On such a basis the nerve specialist would frequently be able to make the right and helpful diagnosis without the aid of any "confession" and without awakening in the patient the slightest suspicion that his physician had discovered the real source of the trouble. Experiments have convinced me that the method may bring to light facts of which even the patient himself is ignorant. Ideas which are connected in his deepest soul, but which he cannot bring up voluntarily by mere effort of memory, are sometimes brought to expression by the mechanical devices of this association method. It seems that as soon as a number of associations have been produced under pressure of the desire to associate as quickly as possible, the mind enters into a state of decreased inhibition, in which suppressed and forgotten ideas rush forward.

This fact must become the more important, the more we learn, under the guidance of the Vienna School, that one of the most troublesome nervous diseases — namely, hysteria — results principally from suppressed affective ideas, and can be cured by awaking anew the restrained thought. Hysteria is "strangulated emotion," and disappears when the forgotten emotional ideas are brought to conscious expression. One hysteric woman always became mute after sunset; another could not take any food but liquids; another was constantly tortured by the hallucination of the tobacco odour. Every physician knows a hundred such hysteric symptoms. No one of these patients knew the reason or origin of her trouble. Slowly the physician discovered the suppressed ideas, which had had no chance to express themselves and had worked disaster in their inhibited form. The woman who could not speak at night had sat once at sunset years before, at the bedside of her sick father; she had vehemently suppressed every sound in order not to disturb him. As soon as this first scene was brought back to her mind, she regained her voice. The woman who could not take solid food had been obliged, years before, to suppress her disgust when eating at the same table with a man who suffered from an ugly disease. As soon as this starting-point was consciously associated again, she was ready to dine like others. The woman who smelled tobacco had long before heard by chance, in a room full of smoke, that the man she loved was in love with another, and she had had to suppress her emotion on account of the presence of others.

As soon as she connected the smell again in consciousness with that first strangulated emotion, the hallucination disappeared. Hysteric contractions and anæsthesias, pathological impulses and inhibitions, can all be removed if the long-forgotten emotional ideas with which the disturbance started can be brought to light. Just here the association method seems sometimes helpful. The psychologist who seeks to discover the secret connections of ideas may thus, by his association method, not only protect the innocent and unmask the guilty, but bring health and strength to the nervous wreck.

Yet our chief interest belongs to the legal aspect of this method. Carried out with the skill which only long laboratory training can give, it has become, indeed, a magnifying-glass for the most subtle mental mechanism, and by it the secrets of the criminal mind may be unveiled. All this has, of course, no legal standing to-day, and there is probably no one who desires to increase the number of "experts" in our criminal courts. But justice demands that truth and lies be disentangled. The time will come when the methods of experimental psychology cannot longer be excluded from the court of law. It is well known that the use of stenographers in trials once met with vehement opposition, while now the shorthand record of the court procedure seems a matter of course. The help of the psychologist will become not less indispensable. The vulgar ordeals of the "third degree" in every form belong to the Middle Ages, and much of the wrangling of attorneys about technicalities in admitting the "evidence" appears to not a few somewhat out of date, too: the methods of experimental psychology are working in the spirit of the twentieth century. The "third degree" may brutalise the mind and force either correct or falsified secrets to light; the time-measurement of association is swifter and cleaner, more scientific, more humane, and more reliable in bringing out the truth which justice demands. Of course, we are only at the beginning of its development; the new method is still in many ways imperfect, and if clumsily applied it may be misleading; moreover, there exists no hard and fast rule which fits every case mechanically. But all this indicates only that, just as the bodily facts have to be examined by the chemist or the physiologist, the mental facts must be examined also, not by the layman, but by the scientific psychologist, with the training of a psychological laboratory.

5

The Traces of Emotions

If a girl blushes when a boy's name is mentioned in the family sitting-room, we feel sure, even if she protests, that he is not quite indifferent to her young heart. If she opens a letter and grows pale while reading it, she may assure us that the event is unimportant; we know better. If she talks with you and every word makes you believe that her entire interest belongs to you and your remarks, it is enough for you to see that her fingers are playing nervously with her fan, and that her breathing has become deep and vehement and her eyes restless since a certain guest has entered the room; you know she is hardly listening to you and waits only for him to approach her. And if he does not come, — she may be masterful in simulation and the artificial smile may never leave the lips, yet you will hear her disappointment in the timbre of her voice, you may see it even in the width of the pupil of her eye.

Yes, the hidden feeling betrays itself often against the will of the best comedian in life. It may be easy to suppress intentionally the conspicuous movements by which we usually accentuate the emotions. It is not necessary to become wild with anger and to collapse in sorrow, we may even inhibit laughter and tears, and a New Englander will never behave like a Southern Italian. But the lips and hands and arms and legs, which are under our control, are never the only witnesses to the drama which goes on inside — if they keep silent, others will speak. The poets know it well. Through the dramatic literature of all ages is repeated the motive of the unintentional expression of emotions. The ghastly memory of a gruesome past seems locked up in the hero's mind; and yet when he is brought back to the place of his deed, it comes to light in his paleness and trembling, in the empty glaring of his eyes and the breaking of his voice. There is hardly a tragedy of Shakespeare in which the involuntary signs of secret excitement do not play their rôle. And the comedies of all time vary the same motive with regard to the lighter sins of love and social entanglement. The helpless stammering of the excited lover betrays everything which his deliberate words are to deny.

But the signs which made Hamlet sure that his mother had committed murder have not been overlooked by those who are on the track of the criminal in our practical life. The suspected man who pales before the victim while he pretends not to know him, or who weeps at hearing the story of the crimes which he disavows, is half condemned in the eyes of the prosecutor. When the conspiracy against Dreyfus sought to manufacture evidence against him, they made much of the fact that he trembled and was thus hardly able to write when they dictated to him a letter in which phrases of the discovered treasonable manuscript occurred. Much of that which the police and the delinquents call the third degree consists of these bodily signs of a guilty conscience; to make the accused break down from his own inner emotion is the triumph of such maladministration of law.

It seems that even some of the superstitions of barbaric times which claimed to discover the guilty by all kinds of miracles sometimes contained a certain truth of this kind. They depended on apparently mysterious signs which in reality sometimes belonged to the bodily effects of emotion. Evidently primitive life sharpens the observation of such symptoms. One of the most adventurous "gunmen" of the West told me that when he was attacked by mobs he behaved as if he were constantly spitting; he went through such motions because it always discourages the crowd when they see that their adversary does not fear them, and they would know that a man who is afraid cannot spit — the emotion of fear dries up the mouth and throat.

Of course, everyone knows how uncertain and unsafe such crude police methods must be. There cannot be justice if we base our judgment on the detective's claim that a man blushed or trembled or was breathing heavily. It would hardly be better than those superstitious decisions of early times. There are too many who believe that they see what they expect to see, and very different emotions may express themselves with very similar symptoms. The door is open for every arbitrariness if such superficial observations were to count seriously for acquittal or for conviction. But that provokes the natural question: cannot science help us out? Cannot science determine with exactitude and safety that which is vague in the mere chance judgment of police officers? More than that: cannot science make visible that which is too faint and weak to be noticed by the ordinary observer? The bystander watches the expressions of the strong overwhelming emotions — but can science, can experimental psychology, not bring to light the traces of the whole interplay of feelings, the light and passing ones as well as the strong, and the most hidden suggestions of consciousness as well as heavy emotional storms?

The question is indeed pressing, as the idea of the psychological expert in court cannot be withdrawn from public discussion. The mental life, — perception and memory, attention and thought, feeling and will — plays too important a role in court procedure to reject the advice of those who devote their work to the study of these functions. And especially the progress of modern psychology has been too rapid in recent years to ignore it still with that condescension which was in order at the time when psychologists indulged in speculation and psychological laboratories were unknown. Today the psychologist operates with the methods of exact science, and the method which is here demanded seems entirely in harmony with his endeavours. The problem is whether he can record objectively the passing symptoms and whether he can get hold of expressions too faint to be perceptible to our senses. But just that the laboratory psychologist is aiming at constantly and successfully. Whether he measures the time of mental acts or analyses the complex ideas, whether he studies the senses or the volitions, he is always engaged in connecting the vague inner impression with an outer measurable fact which can be recorded, and in throwing full light on that which escapes notice in ordinary life.

In the region of feelings and emotions the experimental methods of psychology have been certainly not less successful than in other fields of inner life. To confine ourselves to that special problem which interested us from the point of view of law: the psychologist can indeed register the symptoms of inner excitement and, more than that, can show the effects of feelings and emotions of which the mere practical observation does not give us any trace. Yet even the subtlest detective work of the psychological instruments refers only to the same bodily functions which make us visibly blush in shame, pale and tremble in fear, shiver in horror, weep in grief, perspire in anxiety, dance in joy, grow hot and clench the fist in anger. Everywhere the blood vessels contract or dilate, the heart beat changes, the glands increase or decrease their activity, the muscles work irregularly: but the instruments allow us to become aware of almost microscopic changes. We may, perhaps, point to a variety of lines along which such inquiry may move.

To begin with a very simple group of processes, we may start with our ordinary movements is of the arm: does feeling influence them? I can give my reply from a little diary of mine. I kept it years ago. It was not the regulation diary — there was no sentimentality in it, but mostly figures. Its purpose was to record the results of about twenty experiments which took about half an hour's time. I had the material for these little experiments always in my pocket and repeated them three or four times a day throughout several months. I fell to experimenting whenever daily life brought me into a characteristic mental state, such as emotion or interest or fatigue or anything important to the psychologist. One of these twenty experiments was the following: I attached to the bottom of my waistcoat a small instrument which allowed me to slide along an edge between thumb and fore-finger of the right hand, both outwards and inwards. Now I had trained myself to measure off in this way from memory distances of four and eight inches. Under normal conditions my hand passed through these distances with exactitude while the eyes were closed; the apparatus registered carefully whether I made the distance too long or too short. The results of many hundreds of these measurements went into my diary together with a description of the mood in which I was.

When I came to figure up the results after half a year's records I found a definite relation between my feelings and my arm movements. My diary indicated essentially three fundamental pairs of feeling in the course of time. There was pleasure and displeasure, there was excitement and depression, and there was gravity and hilarity. The figures showed that in the state of excitement both the outward and inward movements became too long, and in the state of depression both became too short; in the state of pleasure the outward movements became too long, the inward movements too short; in the state of displeasure the opposite — the outward movements too short and the inward movements too long. In the case of gravity or hilarity no constant change in the length of the movement resulted, but the rhythm and rapidity of the action was influenced by them.

Here were, for the first time, three distinct sets of feelings separated and recognised through three distinct ways of bodily behaviour. After the publication of my figures, others came from other starting points to such division of our feelings into three groups, while some believe that there are only two sets. Still others hold, and I should not disagree, that pleasure and displeasure alone are the fundamental feelings; that a colour or a sound is agreeable seems primary, that it is exciting or soothing is secondary. On the other hand the number of those secondary feelings seems to me to-day still larger than it did at that time; I am inclined to accept many more simple feelings and find for everyone characteristic expressions of movement. All this becomes important as soon as the psychologist begins to explain the feelings and asks how far the sensations themselves enter as parts into the feelings.

But what concerns us here is the fact that the pleasurable and the unpleasurable mood betray themselves in opposite movement —impulses of which we are unaware. I had meant in those hundreds of cases to make exactly the same outward and inward movements and yet the experiments disclosed the illusion. Of course, we all know how in joy the outward movements are reinforced; the boy swings his cap and the whole body stretches itself, while in anger the opposite impulses prevail — the contraction of the fist becomes typical. The experiments show that these various impulses are at work when we do not know and do not show it: we must bring the man before a registering apparatus to find out from his motions without his knowledge whether sunshine or general cloudiness prevails in his mind.

But the unintentional movements may become symptoms of feelings in still a different way. The thing which awakes our feeling starts our actions towards the interesting object. All muscle reading or thought reading works by means of such a principle. The ouija-board of the spiritualists is a familiar instrument for the indication of such impulses, and if we want a careful registering of the unnoticeable movement, we may use an automatograph — a plate which lies on metal balls and thus follows every impulse of the hand which lies flat on it; the plate has an attachment by which the slightest movements are registered on a slowly moving surface. If the arm is held in a loop which hangs from the ceiling, the hand will still more easily follow the weakest impulse without our knowledge. Ask your subject to think attentively of a special letter in the alphabet and then spread twenty-five cards with the letters in a half-circle about him; his arm on the automatograph will quickly show the faint impulse towards the letter of which he thought, although he remains entirely unaware of it. And if a witness or a criminal in front of a row of a dozen men claims that he does not know any one of them, he will point on the automatograph, nevertheless, towards the man whom he really knows and whose face brings him thus into emotional excitement. Still easier may be the graphic record, if it is not necessary to show a definite direction but simply a sudden reaction. The hand may lie on a rubber bulb or on a capsule covered with very elastic rubber and the slightest movement of the fingers will press the air in the capsule which, through a rubber tube, is conducted to a little bulb that pushes a lever and the lever registers its up and down motions. The accused may believe himself to be motionless, and yet when he hears the dangerous name of the place of his crime or of an accomplice, his unintentional muscle contraction will be registered. It is only a question of technique thus to take exact record of the faintest trembling when a little cap is attached to the finger.

The emotional interest may betray itself in an interesting way even through movements which are ordinarily not consciously guided like those of our hands and fingers; I am thinking of the eye movements. I found that our eyes may go their own way without our knowledge. My subject, for instance, looks straight forward; I show him a card with a printed word which is indifferent to him. We have agreed beforehand that after seeing and reading the card he is to close his eyes, to turn his head somewhat sidewards, and then to open his eyes again. The experiment shows that if he does perform these acts, his eyes, after the sideward movement of his head, look in the same direction in which his head points. I repeat this several times; always with the same result. Now I take a card with a word which, I know, is emotionally important to my subject from an earlier experience. The result is suddenly changed: he reads it, closes his eyes, turns his head, opens his eyes again, and, without his knowledge, his eyes have not followed his head but are still turned towards the exciting word — the feeling interest has been betrayed by the unintentional backward rotation of the eye-balls. I may show in this way to the suspected man one indifferent thing after another; his eyes will follow his head. Then I show an object which was instrumental in the crime or which was present at the place of the deed or which belonged to the victim and, if he recognises it, his eyes will stick to it while his head is moving and after. Yes, the police know from old experience that not only do the eyes want to be back at the exciting scene, but the whole man is magnetically drawn to the spot where the crime was committed. Dostojewski shows us how the murderer, almost against his own will, returns to the place of his emotion and thus runs upon his doom.

We are still speaking, of course, of movements and yet of an entirely different process if we consider the breathing. Our inspirations and expirations can be registered in finest detail and a variety of elegant methods are available. Perhaps the simplest "pneumograph" consists of a tube made of spiral wire and covered with rubber, to be attached by ribbons to the chest. Every respiratory movement lengthens and shortens the tube, and this presses a part of the air contained into a little capsule, the cover of which follows the changing pressure of the air and moves a registering lever, usually a large straw which enlarges the movements of the cover. The end of the straw but touches the smoked surface of a slowly revolving drum; it thus writes in the thin layer of smoke a wave line which shows the subtlest features of the breathing. It is a simple task to measure every element of such a curve, every change in the length, in the height, in the angle, in the regularity of the wave; and that means every change in the rapidity, rhythm, distribution, pauses and strength of the breathing. As soon as such delicate methods of registration are applied, the intimate relation between feeling and breath becomes evident. Pleasure, for instance, makes the respiration weaker and quicker; displeasure, stronger and slower; excitement makes it stronger and quicker; acquiescence, weaker and slower. But such generalisations cannot do any justice to the manifoldness of changes that may occur: every ripple on the interests of the mind reflects itself in the changes of the pneumographic wave — it may be an agreeable or disagreeable smell or taste, it may be exciting or depressing news from without or a fancy from within.

The same holds true for the heart beat, measured by the blood wave in the arteries; such a pulse writer is called a sphygmograph. It may be attached, for instance, to the wrist; a delicate lever presses against the wall of the blood vessel just where the finger of the physician would feel the pulse. The lever is attached again to the thin rubber which covers an air chamber, and the changing pressure of air is again transmitted to a long straw which writes an enlarged record of the movement on the revolving drum, rotating regularly by means of clockwork. Here again the height and length and form of every pulse beat may have its own physiognomy. When we write pulse and breathing together on the same drum, we see at once that even every ordinary inspiration changes the pulse; while we inhale we have a pulse different from the pulse while we exhale. Far more influential are the feelings. Again it is only an insufficient abstraction if we generalise and say: pleasure heightens and retards the pulse, displeasure weakens and accelerates it, or excitement makes the pulse stronger and quicker, acquiescence weaker and slower. But there is still another way open to observe the changes in our blood vessels. We may examine the quantity of blood, for instance, which streams to a limb, by means of the so-called plethysmograph. The arm is held by a large tube filled with water; a rubber ring closes the tube. The change of blood supply which makes the arm swell changes the pressure which the water exerts against the air, which is again conducted through a rubber tube to a recording lever; every emotional excitement speaks in the blood supply of every limb. All these instruments of registration have belonged for decades to the household equipment of every physiological laboratory; it was therefore a sad spectacle when recently scores of American papers told their readers that I had invented the sphygmograph and automatograph and plethysmograph this summer — they might just as well have added that I invented the telegraph last spring. To recent years belongs only the application of these instruments for the study of feelings and emotions.

But we may go still further and point to expressions of emotions which are entirely beyond human senses. If we put our hands on two copper plates and make the weak galvanic current of a battery run through the plates and our body, we can, with the help of a delicate galvanometer, measure the slightest variations of the resistance to the current. Experiment shows that such changes occur, indeed, if our brain is excited; any emotional disturbance influences the resistance: it seems that the activity of the sweat-glands in the skin is under the nervous influence of our feelings, and the functioning of these glands alters the electrical conditions. A word we hear may excite us and at once the needle of the galvanometer becomes restless: there is no more uncanny betrayal of our inmost mind. Or we may point to the curious facts of the knee jerk. A little hammer falls always from the same height on the tendon of the knee, and every time the leg makes a jerking reflex movement, the angle of which can be registered. Experiment shows again that this angle changes with the emotional excitement of the mind; evidently the brain sends impulses down to the lower part of the spinal cord where the knee reflex is produced, and the emotion inhibits those messages and changes the whole function. Even the temperature of the body seems to be influenced by excitement; the experienced physician knows how the emotion of the patient can change his feverish state, and experiment seems to indicate similar changes for the normal state.

There is thus really no doubt that experimental psychology

can furnish amply everything which the court demands: it can register objectively the symptoms of the emotions and make the observation thus independent of chance judgment, and, moreover, it can trace emotions through involuntary movements, breathing, pulse, and so on, where ordinary observation fails entirely. And yet, it seems to me that a great reluctance and even a certain scepticism as to the practical application of these methods is still in order. Firstly, the studies in this field of the bodily registration of emotion are still in their beginnings and so far many difficulties are not overcome; there are still contradictions in the results of various scholars. Especially we know too little yet about the evident individual differences to make, for instance, a breathing and pulse curve to-day a basis for a legal condemnation or acquittal. The facts themselves are so complicated that much further work must be done before we can disentangle the practical situations.

Secondly, experiment gives us so far not sufficient hold for the discrimination of the guilty conscience and the emotional excitement of the innocent. The innocent man, especially the nervous man, may grow as much excited on the witness stand as the criminal when the victim and the means of the crime are mentioned; his fear that he may be condemned unjustly may influence his muscles, glands and blood vessels as strongly as if he were guilty. Experimental psychology cannot wish to imitate with its subtle methods the injustice of barbarous police methods. The real use of the experimental emotion-method is therefore so far probably confined to those cases in which it is to be found out whether a suspected person knows anything about a certain place or man or thing. Thus if a new name, for instance, is brought in, the method is reliable; the innocent, who never heard the name before, will not be more excited if he hears that one among a dozen others; the criminal, who knows the name as that of a witness of the crime, will show the emotional symptoms. And yet, it may be rash to propose narrow limits for the practical use, as the rapid progress of experimental crimino-psychology may solve to-morrow those difficulties which seem still to stand in the way to-day.

6
Untrue Confessions

It is a sad story which I am going to report, a weird tragedy of yesterday. I am most seriously convinced that it is a tragedy not only of crime but also of human error and miscarried justice, and my scientific conscience as a psychologist compels me to speak of it because the tragedy of yesterday may come up again, in some other form, to-morrow.

I am the last one to desire for the modern psychologist a special privilege to meddle with the daily affairs of practical life. Far too often the "new" psychology has been made a kind of Jack-of-all-trades. Psychology has had to furnish the patent medicine for all the defects of our schools, psychology has become the word to conjure with in literature and religion, in social troubles and economic emergencies, and the public can hardly imagine how a psychologist's mail is burdened with inquiries from superstitious and unbalanced minds and with reports of uncanny and mysterious happenings. Wherever experience seems unexplainable, the psychologist is expected at least to pigeon-hole and to label the occurrence and to give his official sanction that such strange things may sometimes happen. Yet, the psychologist can hardly glance over such letters without wishing that the public at least might know how much wiser it would be to consult a detective. No mental explanation is in order till the facts themselves are cleared up by methods for which the scholar is not prepared at all. His steady contact with seekers for truth makes him least suspicious of the thousand sources of delusion and deception which an attorney may find out, but not a scholar.

But if the psychologist has thus not seldom the wish that the detective were consulted in his place, that does not prevent his regretting sometimes that the world relies on the detective instead of calling in the psychologist. The more the scientific analysis and explanation of mental life makes progress through the experimental and physiological, comparative and clinical methods, the more we learn how subtle the internal connections are and how insufficient the popular psychology must be with which the facts of life are usually interpreted by detectives and attorneys, by juries and judges. To be sure, they all respect the physician who examines whether the criminal was insane or mentally disordered. But between the common-sense of the average juryman and the medical science of the alienist the world of criminal facts cannot be divided fairly. The detective may bring out much evidence which lies outside of the realm of physicians, which yet may be a closed book to the naïve view of psychical life. In such case the psychologist feels it his duty fearlessly to oppose the popular prejudice.

Just this was the situation when I ventured last year to write a letter to a well-known nerve specialist in Chicago who had privately asked my opinion as a psychologist in the case of a man condemned to death for murder. The man had confessed the crime. Yet I felt sure that he was innocent. My letter somehow reached the papers and I became the target for editorial sharp-shooters everywhere. I have before me still a collection of such specimens. "Harvard's Contempt of Court" is the big heading here, "Science Gone Crazy" the heading there, and so it went on in the papers, while every mail brought an epistolary chorus. The efforts of the attorneys to change the condemned man's fate by a motion for a supersedeas before the Supreme Court were unsuccessful. One week later the accused was hanged; yet, if scientific conviction has the right to stand frankly for the truth, I have to say again that he was hanged for a crime of which he was no more guilty than you or I, and the only difference which the last few months have brought about is the fact that, as I have been informed on good authority, the most sober-minded people of Chicago to-day share this sad opinion.

I felt sure from the first that no one was to be blamed. Court and jury had evidently done their best to find the facts and to weigh the evidence; they are not to be expected to be experts in the analysis of unusual mental states. The proof of the alibi seemed sufficient to some, but insufficient to others; most various facts allowed of different interpretation, but all hesitation had to be overcome by the one fundamental argument which excluded every doubt: there was a complete confession. And if the sensational press did not manifest a judicial temper, that seemed this time very excusable. The whole population had been at the highest nervous tension from the frequency of brutal murders in the streets of Chicago. Too often the human beast escaped justice: this time at last they had found the villain who confessed — he at least was not to escape the gallows. For many years no murder case had so deeply excited the whole city. Truly, as long as a demand for further psychological inquiry appeared to the masses simply as "another way of possibly cheating justice" and as a method tending "towards emasculating court procedure and discouraging and disgusting every faithful officer of the law," the newspapers were almost in duty bound to rush on in the tracks of popular prejudice.

I took it thus gladly as a noble outburst of Chicago feeling against my "long-distance impudence" that a leading paper resumed the situation in this way: "Illinois has quite enough of people with an itching mania for attending to other people's business without importing impertinence from Massachusetts. This crime itself, no matter who may be the criminal, was one of the frightful fruits of a sickly paltering with the stern administration of law. We do not want any directions from Harvard University irresponsibles for paltering still further." This seems to me to hit the nail on the head exactly, and my only disagreement is with the clause "no matter who may be the criminal." I think it does matter who may be the criminal — whether the one whom they hanged or somebody else who is still to-day in freedom.

But if I examine these endless reports for a real argument why the accused youth was guilty of the heinous crime, everything comes back after all to the statement constantly repeated that it would be "inconceivable that any man who was innocent of it should claim the infamy of guilt." Months have passed since the neck of the young man was broken and "thousands of persons crowded Michigan Street, jamming that thoroughfare from Clark Street to Dearborn Avenue, waiting for the undertaker's wagon to leave the jail yard." The discussion is thus long since removed to the sphere of theoretical argument; and so the hour may be more favourable now for asking once more whether it is really "inconceivable" that an innocent man can confess to a crime of which he is wholly ignorant. Yet the theoretical question may perhaps demand no later than to-morrow a practical answer, when perhaps again a weak mind shall work itself into an untrue confession and the community again rely thereon satisfied, hypnotised by the spell of the dangerous belief that "murder will out." The history of crime in Chicago has shown sufficiently that murder will not "out." It is important that the court, instead of bringing out the guilty thought, shall not bring it "in" into an innocent consciousness.

Of course in a criminal procedure there cannot be any better evidence than a confession, provided that it is reliable and well proved. If the accused acknowledges in express words the guilt in a criminal charge, the purpose of the procedure seems to have been reached; and yet at all times and in all nations experience has suggested a certain distrust of confessions. The earnestness with which caution is urged is decidedly different at different periods; the danger of accepting confessions seems to have been felt more strongly at some times than at others. Has this perhaps depended on the nervous disposition of the crowd at various epochs? No doubt, the abnormal, hysterical, neurotic tendency fluctuated greatly in previous centuries in which the world was scientifically still unaware of its own nervousness and its own hysteria, and yet protected its social life instinctively against its dangers. The essential argument, however, against the trustworthiness of confessions had a purely social origin: it referred to possible promises or threats by other members of the community. No doubt, the chances for such influences were different, too, at various times and in different social conditions. The self-sacrificing desire to exculpate others has played its rôle occasionally also. In short, there is no lack of social motives to make it conceivable from the start that an accused makes of his own accord a confession against himself which is not true. Especially in the realm of the minor offences, promise and threat are still to-day constant sources of untrue self-accusation.

Perhaps we can add still another motive which might induce a man in full possession of his understanding to declare himself guilty against his better knowledge. No statistics can tell the story, but we can suppose that persons suspected wrongly of a crime may, in the face of an unfortunate combination of damaging evidence, prefer to make a false confession in the hope of a recommendation to mercy. Every lawyer knows the famous Boom case in Vermont, where the brothers confessed to having killed their brother-in-law and described the deed in full detail and how they destroyed the body; while long afterwards the "murdered" man returned alive to the village. The evidence against the suspected appeared so overwhelming that they saw only one hope to save their lives — by turning the verdict, through their untrue confession, from murder to manslaughter. To this group we might count not a few of the historic confessions in the Salem witchcraft tragedy. The nearest relatives urged the unfortunate accused women to such confessions, seeing no other way of escape for them.

But just those dark chapters of New England history can show us an abundance of other forms of confession which lead us step for step from well-balanced calculation to complete alienation, through all the borderland regions of mental confusion and disintegration. Even the advice of the nearest relatives of those accused as witches was often not at all based on confidence. The preposterous accusations were for them too sufficient proof of guilt, and not to confess appeared to them as obstinacy. Thus they urged the poor women prisoners, starting from the conviction that the unwillingness to confess showed that their minds were wholly given over to Satan. "In many cases where they yielded, it was not from unworthy fear or for self-preservation, but because their judgment was overthrown and their minds in complete subjection and prostration." There can, indeed, hardly be a doubt that in some instances the confessing persons really believed themselves "guilty." The reports agree further that the accused persons, when they made up their minds to confess, "fabricated their stories with much ingenuity and tact, making them tally with the statements of the accusers, adding points and items that gave an air of truthfulness."

Ann Foster at Salem Village confessed in 1692 that the devil appeared to her in the shape of a bird at several times. She further stated that it was Goody Carrier that made her a witch. "She told her that if she would not be a witch, the devil would tear her to pieces and carry her away — at which time she promised to serve the devil; that she was at the meeting of the witches at Salem Village: they got upon sticks: and went said journey," and so forth. Yet Ann Foster was not insane; the horrors of the accusation had overpowered the distressed mind. We should say to-day that a dissociation of her little mind had set in; the emotional shock brought it about that the normal personality went to pieces and that a split-off second personality began to form itself with its own connected life story built up from the absurd superstitions which had been suggested to her through the hypnotising examinations.

The untrue confessions from hope or fear, through promises and threats, from cunning calculations and passive yielding thus shade off into others which are given with real conviction under the pressure of emotional excitement or under the spell of overpowering influences. Even the mere fatigue often brought to the Salem witches the loosening of the mental firmness and the intrusion of the suggestion of guilt. In tedious examinations the prisoners were urged to confess through many hours "till the accused were wearied out by being forced to stand so long or by want of sleep" and then gave assent to the accusation of having signed the devil's book.

It seems like the other pole of the social world if we turn from these cruel court procedures to the helpful humanity of our hospitals for the insane. But the sounds of reckless untrue self-accusation are familiar there too to everyone who knows the scenes of misery in the ward of the melancholic patients. There is no judge and no jury, only the physician and the nurse, yet no torture of punishment can be harder than the suffering of the melancholic who feels remorse for sins which he never committed, for crimes of which he never thought before. Years ago his friend died; now arises the illusion that he has poisoned him. The last fire in the town was laid by him; he is guilty of the unpardonable sin. The slightest fault in his real past takes, in this illusory affective state, new and gigantic dimensions; long-forgotten mistakes awake with unproportionate feelings of anguish. The patient accuses himself of meanness and deceit, of diabolical plans, and with growing accuracy he elaborates the minute details of his imaginary crimes.

As a matter of course, when the physician speaks in the modern court-room the grave word Melancholia, the self-accusation cannot have any further consequences of a judicial character. The doors of the hospital are closed behind the patient. He may still be witness against others; but the confessions of crime which he claims to have committed himself cannot be considered as evidence under any circumstances. And as the symptoms of melancholia and other depressive states with self-accusatory ideas are easily recognised, there remains hardly any reason for fearing lest such irresponsible fabrications of a diseased brain be taken as real confessions of an actual criminal. But does this give security for a proper rating of those illusory confessions which, like the absurdities of the Salem witches, result from the temporary abnormal states of a not-diseased brain? Hysterical and autohypnotic states may there combine with otherwise perfectly normal behaviour, and pseudo-confessions may thus arise in men who are distinctly not ill. A slight dissociation of mind may set in which does not suggest calling for the physician at all, and which may yet affect profoundly the admissions made by the accused person. Has the court sufficient means at hand to convince the jury that it must weigh all the evidence with a fair consideration of these not pathological, yet very influential, mental variations?

Whether the crime was done in a state of mental responsibility is certainly a question never neglected. The mental status of the witnesses finds usually much less subtle analysis: the cross-examining lawyers turn their attention mostly backwards to the time of the crime and overlook too often the mental state at the time of the trial. But above all, the psychical state of the defendant himself during the trial is usually measured by the crudest standards of easy-going psychology which considers a mental life as typical and unaltered as long as the man is neither insane nor intoxicated. And yet it would be perhaps less exaggerated if we claimed that no psychical mechanism remains entirely unchanged when a witness speaks under his oath or when a defendant faces the jury. The variations remain, of course, mostly within the limits of normal life, as we have to call normal every setting which harmonises with the life purposes of the individual. But variations they are, nevertheless, and only the psychologist may be clearly aware of their tendencies. Practical life would be satisfied with the broad statement that the witness was excited, or anxious and timid, or felt himself important, or was eager to prove his view. How far really his mental possibilities were influenced, how far his perceptions, memory, ideas, imaginative acts, feelings, emotions, volitions, attention, judgment and ideas of self were altered through the situation is not considered and would be certainly unimportant in ninety-nine cases out of a hundred.

Yet we must not forget that there is nowhere a sharp line to be drawn between the symptoms of real mental disease and the variations in normal personalities. There is no mental trait which belongs to mental diseases only; whatever we find in the asylums is made up of the same material that enters into the normal interplay of human minds. The order and harmony alone are disturbed; a single feature is grossly exaggerated or unduly inhibited, and by this abnormal increase or decrease of a regular trait the balance is lost and danger is ahead. Mental diseases are like caricatures of a person; in the caricature too every part of the face is the same as in the ordinary physiognomy, but the proportion is lost, as one special part, perhaps the nose or the teeth are grotesquely enlarged. All mental aberrations are such exaggerated caricatures of the normal feelings, or emotions, or impulses, or memories, or imaginations, or attentions. And because the disease does not develop perfectly new features, but simply reinforces quite ordinary tendencies, it is easy to see that there is nowhere a sharp line between the normal trait and its pathological over-functioning.

The motionless brooding of the melancholic patient is easily recognised, and yet the pessimistic temperament of many a normal man or woman generates all the features which are so sadly developed in the melancholic attacks. Even the self-accusations and the self-destructive despair of the melancholic find their counterpart in the realm of normal life; the pessimist is too often inclined to torture himself by opprobriums, to feel discouraged with himself, and to feel guilty without real guilt. From these slight traces of temperamental type to the complete alienation of the hopeless patient there is a sliding scale of depressions. It leads through all the affective states of the neurasthenic and other neurotic varieties. To recognise where the temperament ends and the irresponsible disturbance begins is made extremely difficult by the great breadth of the borderland region. Public opinion, and court and jury as its organs, are always inclined to claim that whole borderland field still for the normal life and to acknowledge the mental disturbance only when the disease region is entered. But modern psychology recognises daily more strongly that the subtlest analysis of the occurrences in the borderland field is absolutely necessary if the higher ends of social justice are to be reached. The courts show in all other fields that the progress of science breaks new paths for them. It is, for instance, interesting to see how the neurasthenic states are slowly recognised by the courts in civil suits as real bodily disturbance, while a short time ago they were still considered as mere imaginations and illusory complaints. The time has come to take notice of the progress in psychology too.

There is no less a transitional region for all the other mental activities. Everyone knows in daily life the type of the superficial, silly person whose attention is always shifting, and yet it is only an absurd exaggeration of such behaviour that characterises the alienation of the maniac. We know the sanguine type with its quick, sudden impulses, or the slow mind whose will appears always inhibited, as if every volition is checked by an inner resistance. We know the stubborn mind which cannot be persuaded by any logical argument and which sticks to its fixed ideas, and we know the suggestible mind which follows the last hint and believes everything, or at least everything which is printed. Every one of these features of a mental physiognomy may grow till its caricature stands before us as disease, and everywhere there are many steps between the extremes of pleasant originality of character and the saddest mental abeyance. The trait becomes psychologically alarming as soon as the balance is sufficiently destroyed to make the purposes of life impossible. Persons who perhaps doubt in the reality of the outer world may be found in the asylums and on the philosophic platform; whether the doubting mind is a patient or a philosopher shows itself quickly in the consequences: the philosopher includes that doubt within an harmonious life plan, the patient's life is destroyed by his insane doubt.

This steady correspondence between the normal, slight variations and the hopeless disturbances, and the small steps of transition between the extremes are shown perhaps nowhere more clearly than in the field of memory. We differ from one another not only by good and bad retention of our experiences or by good memory for different spheres, the one for names, the other for faces, the one for figures, the other for sounds, but the disturbances and illusions of memory too are most irregular, and just as no two persons have exactly the same face, certainly no two have the same kind of memory. Even unusual varieties may remain still fully within the limit of soundness. I myself, for instance, have absolutely no memory for the mental processes during sleep; in other words, I have never in my life had a dream. When I talk of dreams in my university courses of psychology, I speak of them just as a blind man might speak of colours. Yet, mental processes go on in my sleeping brain as in other men, because my friends have often found that when they wake me up from deep sleep with a question, I invariably give at first an absurd reply full of reminiscences of the foregoing days; but as soon as I am really awake, not the slightest trace of these comes back to my memory. Yet, this rare variety of memory is not an abnormal state, since it cannot interfere with the purposes of my life; and the remainder of mankind is, indeed, rather to be pitied for its dreams, which may bring a confusion of themselves with the real past. If most people were without dreams, the dreamers would have good reason to consult the nerve physicians and their mental state would be pigeonholed in the borderland region between normality and hallucination. Dreams are hallucinations which become harmless only because the impulses to action become ineffective during sleep.

I say that no field shows such a variety in normal limits as the memory, and this refers to its positive features as much as to its negative ones, as much to the remembering as to the forgetting. That we forget, is in itself certainly no defect and no pathological symptom. On the contrary, we could not fulfil the purposes of our life if we did not disburden our memory constantly of superfluous matter. We were lost if we had to keep in memory every face we have seen in the street and every advertisement we have seen in the papers. Our mind has to sift and sift. And we demand from our normal memory even that it follows somewhat our own imagination. We do not care to remember exactly as we experienced the impressions; our perception is full of little blanks which our imaginative memory fills all the time with fitting associations, and when we remember a landscape, we want to have the picture rounded out and do not care whether the wave of the ocean had exactly this curve and whether the tree had just this number of branches. We remember well when we select the material, eliminate some parts worthy of being forgotten, and add from our own imagination other parts well adapted to reproduce the original experience.

But it is evident that this suppressing and supplementing of memory ideas makes us unfit for life when it assumes large proportions. If we cannot remember our previous experience, and if, in addition to it, our own imagination deceives us by the delusion of pseudo-memories, we are of course completely lost in the social world, and the care of the asylum alone can protect us against utter destruction. Yet, who will decide when the limit is reached where we forget and supplement too much: nowhere is the borderland region broader and nowhere more important for the psychology of the court-room. We may move for a long while still in the realm of the normal. It may be pure fatigue which may decrease our resistance against the creeping of deceptive illusions into our memory, Or it may be a simple emotional excitement; no doubt, the mere fact of being on the witness stand awakens in many minds, by its importance and solemnity, an excitement which is especially favourable for opening the memory to suggestions and to confused ideas which group themselves around some ideas with strong feeling tone. Many a memory succumbs even to an impressive or a suggestive question. And more important still is the suggestiveness of the whole situation and especially of its social elements. All that is still normal; there is no education and no art, no politics and no religion without suggestion, and yet suggestion is certainly to a high degree a suppression of objective memory. But slowly all this leads over into the borderland region. Instead of a sound fatigue, there may be an over-fatigue; instead of light emotional excitement, the deep affectional influence of alcohol or drugs; instead of the mild suggestive influence of the teacher and minister, the deep intrusion of the hypnotising physician or of autohypnotisation. All that is not pathological; yet the abnormalities of the memory may have taken in the meantime dimensions which alter entirely the value of the reported recollections.

The untrustworthiness of memory under all such conditions has nothing whatever to do with the intentions and the veracity of the witness. The average man knows anyhow very little of the working of his own mind and his particular variations escape his attention. It is well known how many persons do not know even that they are colour-blind, or that they lack elements of imagination which are natural to others. A colleague once wanted me to hypnotise him because he had just, in his fortieth year, discovered that he had no power of optical remembering; he hoped to get it through hypnosis, and yet he had never missed it until he read of it in a psychological book. And only the other day I was consulted by a young woman who, up to her college days, had not discovered that other persons do not hear voices when they are alone; she had heard them since childhood days and had felt sure that it was everybody's experience. The average person is unfamiliar with his psychical peculiarities and with the varieties and trickeries of his memory. They do not concern the physician either. But the psychological examination furnishes indeed to-day a kind of mental Roentgen rays which illumine the internal happenings.

We must not forget, moreover, that our knowledge of our own personality and its doing is also only a function of memory. We know of ourselves, in a psychological sense, through the connected memory of our actions and of our experiences, and this reproducing self-consciousness is open to all the chances and defects which belong to our remembering in other fields. Our own doings, of which we know, perhaps, through our muscle sensations, are in themselves no better material for our reproduction in memory than the scenes which we have seen and the words which we have heard. As soon as the memory for our own past is completely lost, the pathological character is, of course, evident; and if the ideas which form our selves become dissociated and groups become split off as a second or third personality in us, no one doubts that such curious formations belong to the physician's domain. Yet here again we can reach the most hopeless forms through small steps from the experiences of our daily life. Every one of us is a different personality under different circumstances.

The man in the office is not the man in family life; on his vacation trip, not the same as at work; in the political meeting, not the same as in the theatre. New leading impulses, new groups of memory associations, new groups of feelings enter each time into play and change the whole aspect of our life. To be sure, the core of our personality is not touched by such daily occurrences, and we can easily bridge over in our mind from the one state to the other. Just for this reason it does not interfere with the purposes of healthy action. But this growing up of a new personality, with its own impulses and separated by its own memories from our regular life, may again increase just like those other variations of memory. An emotional shock or a captivating impression may stir up long-forgotten memory ideas or push imaginative thoughts into the centre and build around them split-off pieces of a dissociated mind into a new personality which can be, perhaps, hardly discriminated from the previous self, but in which important emotions and memories may be distorted. And this alteration may affect more and more the deeper layers of emotional thought and the whole man may be for a long time a new man before the outside becomes aware of it, or before he himself can explain the sudden changes in his attitudes and in his actions, in his judgments and his self-consciousness. The borderland region between the normal variations of personality and the complete pathological destruction of the self demand thus the most earnest consideration in the court-room.

And now I return to the distressing case of Chicago. Dr. Christison has set forth the entire murder case in a brilliant pamphlet which few will study without becoming convinced that an innocent man has suffered death by the rope on account of untrue confessions. It may be sufficient here to cite from it the following facts: On January 12, 1906, a young married woman was brutally outraged and murdered in Chicago. Her body was found, by the unfortunate defendant, lying face downwards on a manure pile in a barnyard. The barn was about half a block distant from his home. He had to go there to attend to his father's horse. When he observed the body, he at once reported the matter to his father at the house, and the father notified the police. The officers who inspected the premises found the woman's hat at her feet, but could discover no evidence whatsoever of a scuffle having taken place. Purse, shopping-bag and muff were gone. Around her neck was a hard-drawn copper wire, the ends being twisted together.

The young man looked as if he had not slept during the night and the officers suspected him. The testimonies show that the young man was everywhere regarded as a thoughtful, obliging fellow of exceptionally good disposition, but often exhibiting marked stupidity. He never sought the company of women. All of his friends thought him decidedly trusting and credulous and absent-minded. He alternated between gay and morose moods. His most pronounced defect seemed to them his lack of initiative. His regular work was with his father at the trade of carpenter. When he came to the police station, he was told at once that he was the guilty man; but the accused denied everything.

Now the police began to press him and to suggest more and more impressively to him his guilt. Suddenly he began to confess, and he was quite willing to repeat his confession again and again. Every time it became richer in detail. "At about 6.30 I took her in the alley. I wrestled with her and lost my senses. She wanted to run," — and so on and so on. On this basis he was condemned to death. So the matter stood when my opinion was asked for, as above reported. I could not help becoming convinced that all the external signs spoke against the interpretation of the jury. The young man's alibi proof, brought forward by his friends, seemed to me convincing. Everything seemed to point to the fact that the woman was murdered by an unknown person at another place, and that her body was dragged during the night by the copper wire coiled around her neck from another street to the barnyard. The so-called "confessions" themselves seemed absurd and contradictory and exactly like the involuntary elaboration of a suggestion put into the man's mind. His whole life history and the expression of his face were in fullest accordance with the suspicion that his mind was in a state of dissociation when he began his confessions. It seemed to me a typical case of that large borderland region in which a neurotic mind develops an illusory memory as to its own doings in the past. After most careful scrutiny as far as the written and printed material allowed, I wrote thus in June in my much-abused letter that the confessions must be untrue and that the condemned man had really nothing to do with the crime. I added at once, "It is an interesting case of dissociation and auto-suggestion; it would need probably careful treatment to build up his dissociated mind again and thus to awake in him a clear memory of his real experiences."

But when I expressed thus my firm conviction, I had, nevertheless, the uncanny feeling that there was something obscure in the case. I was unable to understand how the sudden change from denial to confession was brought about. To be sure, there were the sharp inquisitory questions of the police officers, and yet from a rather extended experience I could not imagine that without a sudden external shock or some overwhelming fascination such a conversion and such a disintegration could set in. Only a short time before a lady had come to me who showed quite similar blanks of memory for several days, filling the gap with imaginative ideas, and she too did not understand why her personality had been changed so suddenly. But when I hypnotised her, I understood what had happened. She had been in a nervous and over-fatigued state when her own physician bent over her, and the sharp sunlight reflected from his eye-glasses struck her eyes. At that moment she felt it like a shock, his eye-glasses seemed to become large and uncanny, and from that moment on her consciousness was split and her remaining half-personality developed a pseudo-memory of its own.

I had before my mind also the case of a certain religious conversion which Dr. Prince has recently analysed and described. It was the case of a young woman who, from a most distressed, restless and suffering state, was suddenly completely changed to a state of joyful excitement and happy ecstasy. She felt it as a spiritual "conversion" to health, and the complete change of her mental personality was indeed most surprising. She could not remember that anything had happened which might have influenced her; but when the physician hypnotised her in the interest of her ailments, everything became clear. She had gone to church in a condition of hopeless despair. The church was empty and, as she communed with herself, her hopelessness deepened. Then her eyes became fixed upon one of the shining brass lamps in the church, and of a sudden all was changed. She went into a trance-like state in which many disconnected memories of her early life and of happy times rushed to her consciousness, each accompanied by emotion, and these long-forgotten emotions of happiness persisted.

If there had been anything of such optical captivation of attention, like the reflex of the eye-glass or the shining of the brass lamp, in the Chicago case, everything would have been completely clear to me; without such fascinating stimulus, I could not account sufficiently for the suddenness of the change in the defendant's personality. When I wrote my letter, I felt certain that if I had had a chance to hypnotise the condemned man, I should have found out that some unexpected stimulus must have come in, must have snapped off the normal connections. I expressed this as my wish at that time, repeatedly. I could not foresee that all the explanation I was looking for would be furnished only a few days later by Nature herself. The unfortunate youth awoke suddenly from the awful spell. The period of disintegration was suddenly again eliminated from the memory and the normal connections entered again into play. The same paper, which had insisted that the defendant must be the murderer because no innocent man would ever confess such a brutal crime, brought out a few days later a long report which began as follows:

"With death on the gallows only six days away, he asserts his innocence of the atrocious murder. He declares he has absolutely no memory of having made to the police a confession . . . He asserts that his only recollection of the coroner's inquest is that of seeing a revolver pointed at him. He said, 'I saw the flash of steel in front of me. Then two men got before me. I can remember no more than that about it. Someone told me afterward who the man was; but I had not seen him at all and I don't recall seeing any other men even until after I had seen the revolver. I suppose I must have made those statements, since they all say I did. But I have no knowledge of having made them, and I am innocent of that crime. From the time that I was arrested I do not believe that I was myself for a moment, until after I was over here in the jail. Everything about that time is a blur, a blank, to me. I can see through this blur the time in the station, when the police would bring me up every little while and tell me that I had done it. I know that the very first thing that the Inspector said to me when I was brought to him was, 'You did this.' I did not do it, and I knew that I did not; but I do not know what I said or did during that time in the station. I wondered why a revolver should be pointed at me,'" and so forth.

It would be absurd to fancy that this last turn of his mind was a made-up story to escape punishment. Through all those weeks of his half-dazed condition, he had never made the least effort to weaken his so-called confessions or to protect himself in any way. Moreover, this stupid boy would be the last to be able to invent suddenly a long story which fits so exactly in every detail the clinical experiences of the nervous physician and the mental experiences of the psychologist. "I saw the flash of steel in front of me." And from that moment everything became a blur and a blank. It was the one missing link in the chain of evidence of his innocence. He cannot even have understood that this flash of steel worked like the shining brass lamp in Dr. Prince's case or the reflecting eye-glass in that other case. He naïvely reported the whole truth, and with all the ear-marks of truth. He would have been absolutely unable to fabricate by his own efforts such scientifically exact observations. What resulted when he begun to fabricate out of his own faculties was sufficiently shown in his " confessions," a contradictory mixture of improbable and psychologically impossible occurrences. Six days later the punishment of death was executed.

7
Suggestions in Court

It was in a large city which I was visiting for the first time. I went to see the hypnotic experiments of a friend, a physician for nervous diseases. He invited me to witness the treatment of a lady who had been deeply hypnotised by him for a local nervous disturbance. Her mind seemed normal in every respect. She was a woman of wealth and social position. When she was in hypnotic sleep, he suggested to her to return in the afternoon when she would find us both, and, as soon as he took out his watch, to declare her willingness to make a last will in which I should become the only heir to all her property. She had never seen me before and I was introduced to her under a fictitious, indifferent name. When she left the office after awakening from her hypnotic sleep, she did not take any notice of me at all. At the appointed hour she returned, apparently not knowing herself why she came. She found in the parlour, besides her physician and me, three or four others who wanted to watch the development of the experiment. She was not embarrassed. She said that she had passed the house by chance and that she thought it would be nice to show her doctor how much better she felt and to ask whether there was any objection to her going to the theatre. I then began a conversation with her about the opera. We talked for perhaps ten minutes on music and the drama, exactly as if we had met at any dinner party, and there was nothing in the least strange in her ideas or in her expression of them.

Suddenly my friend asked how late it was and, as arranged, took his watch out of his pocket. There was a moment of hesitation. The lady spoke the next few words in a stammering way; but then she rushed on and told us that she had not expected to find such a company, but that her real purpose in coming was to report to me that she had selected me as her heir and that now she wanted accordingly to make her last will. Up to this moment her action has been a mechanical carrying out of the post-hypnotic suggestion, but the really interesting part was now to begin. I told her that there must be a mistake, as she could not have seen me before, and I mentioned a fictitious city in which I claimed to live. At once she replied that she had just spent the last winter in that city, and that she had met me there daily on the street, and that from the first she had planned to leave me all that she owned. I insisted that at least she had never spoken to me. Yes, in that same city she had met me repeatedly in society. I represented to her the unnaturalness of leaving her wealth to a stranger instead of to her children. At once she replied that she had thought it out for years, that it would be a blessing for the children not to be burdened with riches, while she knew that I would use them in a philanthropic way. The others took part in the conversation, scores of arguments were brought up to discourage her from this fantastic plan. For each one she had a long-considered excellent rejoinder.

Finally, I told her directly that, as she knew, she had been hypnotised that morning and that this whole idea of the last will had been planted in her head by the witnessed suggestion of her physician. With a charming smile she replied that she knew all that perfectly well, but that she did not contradict and resist this proposition of the doctor simply because it by chance coincided entirely with her own cherished plans, which had been perfectly firm in her mind for a year. She would have written to me some day soon if I had not come to town. She went on that she was unwilling to hear any further doubts of her sincerity and that she was ready to take an oath that she had made up her mind in favour of such a testament long before she was hypnotised. To put an end to all this, she insisted that paper be brought to her, and then she wrote a codicil which left all her property to the fictitious man from the fictitious town. The doctors present had to sign as witnesses. I put the paper into my pocket, switched the conversation over to the theatre again, and, after a few minutes, she had evidently forgotten the whole episode. She treated me again as a complete stranger; and when I asked whether she happened to know the city before mentioned, I was told that she had once passed through it on the train. When she left the house, she had clearly not the slightest remembrance of that document in my pocket, which we others then burned together.

If I had been present as an uninformed stranger during that afternoon visit, I should have been so completely misled that I could not have thought of any additional inquiry or any further argument to test the validity of the testimony. Everything seemed to harmonise with the one plan which had been put into her mind. All her memories became falsified, all her tastes and emotions were turned upside down, all her life experiences were mingled with and supplemented by untrammelled imagination, coupled with the strongest feeling of certainty and sincerity, and yet everything was moulded by her own mind, with the exception of that one decision which had been urged upon her from the outside.

If a suggestion planted in a consciousness would remain there isolated, it would be easy to detect it. It would be in such manifold contradiction with all the normal reminiscences and habitual arguments that every court, for instance, would quickly recognise the strange thought as an intruder. But just this is the uncanny power of suggestion, that it at once infects all the neighbouring ideas and emotions and forces the whole mental life of the personality under the unnatural influence.

Of course, life does not often make such effective experiments, and the danger seems small that judges or jurymen should ever be deceived by such an elaborate performance of a witness. Few persons only can be hypnotised to the degree that a post-hypnotic suggestion becomes so powerful. But it cannot be emphasised too strongly that the extreme abnormal changes in mental life go over by the smallest steps into the perfectly normal and habitual behaviour. The grotesque destructiveness of such a hypnotic revolution shows only an exaggerated form of the dangerous working of suggestion which leads in a sliding scale down to the little bits of strange influences with their unreasonable reasoning, as when we read in the cars the unhypnotic suggestions of "cook with gas" or "read the *sun*" or " wear rubber heels."

The psychologist does not need, indeed, the hypnotic state to demonstrate experimentally how every suggestion contaminates the most sincere memory. A picture of a farmer's room was shown to about forty persons, children and adults. Each one examined it individually and was then asked to give a report from the fresh memory image in reply to detailed questions. The picture had plenty of detail which could easily be grasped. The questions were partly indifferent and objective. How many persons are in the room? Does the room have windows? What is the man doing? There were persons and windows and the man was eating his soup. But other questions, referring to objects not present in the picture, could pass through different stages of suggestiveness. Is there a stove in the room? Is not so intense a suggestion as the express question, did you see the stove in the room? There was no stove in the picture. Are there houses to be seen through the windows of the room? Does a lamp hang from the ceiling? The result showed that the replies to these suggestive questions were correct only in fifty-nine per cent of all cases. Hundreds of times objects were invented in accordance with the suggestion of the question and this immediately after the direct observation of the picture, and without any personal interest in the falsified result.

The experiments show that the resistance for the young people is much weaker than for the grown-ups, for the girls weaker than for the boys, but they all were under perfect conditions of emotional calmness. Such conditions are not to be found on the witness stand under the excitement of the solemn court procedure; there the resistance of the adult persons may sink to the low level of that of the boys and girls. Above all, the experiments show that at all ages the positive effect of the suggestion works itself out in minute and concrete detail. As soon as the subject has answered that there is a stove in the room, he is at once ready to reply by a positive statement to the further question, where is the stove standing? The one says on the left, the other on the right; one in the corner, and one against the middle of the wall, each simply following the path of least resistance in his own imagination. The experiments allowed a complete gradation of the suggestive power of the various questions. The gown of the farmer's wife was red. It was sufficient to ask whether the gown was blue or green to eliminate for many the red entirely from memory. And with the suggestiveness of the question the readiness to elaborate their own inventions steadily increased. Experiments of this kind have been carried on with almost identical results in different nations with persons of different ages and professions with most varied material, and every time the power of a suggestive question to break down the true memory appears alarming. But whoever has studied these protocols of the psychological laboratories cannot help feeling that many cross-examinations in court are only continuations of the interesting tests carried on to demonstrate that there is nothing more suggestive for some persons than a skillful question. Their influence may set in long before the lawyer of the other side rejects a too clumsy suggestion as an unallowed "leading question."

Of course, the illusory effect of a suggestion need not wait till the labour of the memory sets in. Our perceptions themselves may be distorted through suggestive influences. Experimental psychology can demonstrate it and at the same time test it in a thousand forms. Of course, such little psychological laboratory experiments seem petty and far removed from the reality of life experience, as they can offer nothing but a dry schematic pattern. Yet this is a complete misunderstanding. Not the weakness of the experiments but their strength lies in their schematic character. All the experimental sciences teach us to understand the world by bringing its manifoldness to the simplest formula. The physicist too does not wait till the lightning breaks through the clouds; he does not need the thunder storm. The small electrical machine on his laboratory table can teach him in a much more instructive way what factors determine the electric discharge. The artificial schematisation shows the connections between cause and effect alone. Thus we do not need in the laboratory the erratic play of emotions and prejudices which suggestions and persuasions may stir up in the chaos of practical life. We recognise the essential features just as well in the slight changes of perceptive judgment with the tiny material of our workshop.

If I have, for instance, on the one side of my table thirty little squares of grey paper and on the other side the same number of the same material, and I ask the subject to decide without counting on which of the two sides there are more of the grey squares, I can easily arrange that he sees more on whichever side I want him to. I find, perhaps, that his judgment depends upon the grouping, that those thirty pieces suggest different numbers according as they lie in regular lines or in irregular disorder; according as they are shut off in small groups or grouped in one circle; surrounded by a frame, or accentuated by a few ink spots, or brightened by a light background, — in short, that very various side factors suggest an erroneous judgment as to the number of the perceived things. And yet such harmless experimental tests unveil all the factors with which, for instance, political parties before election awake misleading suggestions as to the relative strength of the party vote. A little bit of bright colour on my laboratory table gives me all the moral effect on my subjects which the most wonderful torchlight processions and brass bands can have on the suggestive voter.

Or take a still more striking experiment. We have a series of cardboard boxes of different sizes, from a width of a few inches to several feet, and we make them all exactly equal in weight, filling the smallest, perhaps, with iron and the largest with straw. All are to have the same handle, and if one after the other is lifted with closed eyes, all of course appear of equal heaviness. But now the subject is to lift them, one after the other, with open eyes, and the impression of weight will at once be controlled by the suggestion given by the size. The small box appears now several times heavier than the large one, and no effort to overcome the suggestion can rule out the illusion. It may be a long way from the overestimation of the weight of a little cardboard box to the falsifying overestimation of a piece of evidence by the jury of a murder case, but it is a straight way without demarcation lines. If the twelve jurymen were grouped according to their suggestibility, from the most stubborn to the most easily influenced, they would stand probably in the same order as if they were tested for errors in the judgment of our boxes of cardboard. Yes, we might simplify our test still more. Sometimes I found it sufficient to show to my subjects various pairs of circles drawn on paper; they had to decide which of the pairs was the larger. The pairs were always of the same size, but in their centres various figures were printed; the suggestible person is easily inclined to call the circle with the figure 79 larger than the circle which contains merely the figure 32, just as there may be men who think the prettier girl to be the cleverer, or the richer fellow the more brilliant.

What does the psychologist really understand by a suggestion? Let us be sure from the first that it certainly means nothing abnormal or pathological. The illustrations have indicated sufficiently that abnormal disturbance and ordinary normal life can meet here. My lady with the over-generous last will had certainly left the realm of normality; the voter who is imposed on by the big parade, or the customer who is carried away by the bargain prices of the great removal sale, is also under the influence of suggestion and may yet be otherwise quite a normal person. Suggestion is, moreover, no symptom of weakness, and it would be absurd to believe that life might be wholesomer and better if it could move on without the aid of influences of suggestion. On the contrary, life would be dreary and commonplace, without enthusiasm and without convictions, if all suggestions evaporated. Education and art, politics and religion, rely on the power of suggestion, for a suggestion is after all any idea which takes hold of our consciousness in such a way that it inhibits and excludes the opposite ideas.

But in what sense is there any meaning in speaking of opposite ideas? Our consciousness has room for any combination of thoughts, and each idea seems to go peacefully together with any other idea. We can think black and white and summer and winter and man and woman quietly together. When the psychologist speaks of opposite ideas, he means something very different. He calls opposite such ideas as involve mutually exclusive attitudes. I can think of man and of woman, but I cannot take the attitude towards a person of taking him for a man and at the same time the attitude of taking him for a woman. I can think of summer and winter, but I must believe that the season is either winter or summer, not both, and must act accordingly. The whole antagonism thus lies in our own activities, and, if we say that one idea excludes the opposite, we really mean that the idea which demands one attitude excludes another idea which demands an opposite attitude. In ordinary life, in states free from suggestion, no idea has any prerogative. Each has fair play. When a new idea comes to our mind, perhaps from hearing it from a friend, perhaps from reading it, perhaps from our own imagination, it may fall into a conflict of attitudes with some other idea present and, above all, with some associations and memories which awake; then begins a fair fight in which either the newcomer or the old idea may win; both together cannot last, as we cannot live through opposite actions at the same time: we cannot turn to the right and to the left, we cannot close the hand and open it, we cannot speak and be silent.

Wrong ideas and inappropriate propositions enter our consciousness through many doors all the time, but they are at once eliminated through the influence of the opposite ideas which a faithful memory and a sound reasoning provide. That which is connected most firmly with the remainder of our experience will survive. Each of the rivalling ideas is thus backed by its own connections and stands on its own merits. Whenever this is changed, and an idea, it may be the new intruder or the old incumbent, gets an unfair chance so that all its opposing ideas are weakened and perhaps even suppressed from the start, then we call it a suggestion. All our prejudices and all our convictions work as such suggestions. They do not give to the idea of opposite attitude the opportunity for a test. That may work for the good or for the bad. The moral idea and the vicious desire may be equally strengthened through such suggestive energy which eliminates the opposite from the start. We call the readiness to receive such suggestions from other persons suggestibility. The degree of suggestibility changes from man to man and changes in every individual from mood to mood, from hour to hour. Hypnotism, finally, is an artificially increased state of suggestibility. Yet there are nowhere sharp demarcation lines. Even the most stubborn mind is open to certain suggestions and even the most deeply hypnotised mind has still the power to resist certain ideas which would be opposed by the deepest maxims of his life. Emotion certainly increases suggestibility with everybody; so does fatigue and nervous exhaustion.

There is nothing mysterious in all this, and the psychologist is not unable to understand it all as product of the brain mechanism. He knows to-day that each idea is composed of sensations which accompany nervous excitement in many sensorial brain cells and these are stimulated by the sense organs. But he knows further that this excitement does not stop in those sensory cells. The process which starts from the sense organs does not find in those sensory brain centres an end station, but runs on into motor paths which lead, finally, to the muscular system. Those central brain stations thus serve for the transmission of the incoming sensory stimuli into outgoing motor impulses. All this is endlessly complex. Millions of paths lead to the brain and millions of paths lead out again, and the cortex of the brain is the great automatic switch-board for all those tracks. Yet all this alone would be no explanation. It would make us only understand that any sensory idea, a word which we hear, a thing which we see, would necessarily lead over into an action. But plenty of facts speak now in favour of the following view.

Firstly, those motor paths in the brain are so related to each other that whenever excitement goes on in the one, the track which would lead to the opposite action becomes blocked. When the impulse runs into those nerves which, for instance, open the hand, the brain closes those channels of motor discharge which would lead us to clench the fist. Secondly, the ideas which accompany the sensory brain processes become vivid only when the channels of discharge are open; they remain unvivid, that is, they become inhibited and suppressed when those channels of discharge are closed. A suggestion would thus be an idea whose sensory brain accompaniment keeps the channels of motor discharge wide open, so that the paths which would lead to the opposite action are, on the whole, closed; and because the channels of discharge are closed, all the ideas which might lead to such opposite action are eliminated from the first. If the words, "This is a garden," spoken to me here in my library, came as a suggestion, they would not exclude any activity of mine. I might carry on a conversation on politics, might read a book, and might remember correctly all that happened to me before, but everything must remain in harmony with my attitude towards this room as a garden. The wish to take a book from the shelf on the wall would be indeed inhibited and the books themselves would become correspondingly invisible, while I should believe I saw the flowers in the garden, which I should feel ready to pick. Of course, to take my library shelves for flower bushes because someone tells me this is a garden demands an extreme degree of suggestibility, and, where it is reached, we should certainly speak of an hypnotic state. To take in an anxious mood at twilight the trunk of a willow tree for a burglar requires much less suggestibility; and to believe the latest news of the yellow journal only because it is shouted in big headlines, in spite of the fact that a hundred earlier experiences ought to suppress belief, a still smaller degree of suggestibility is sufficient.

If, therefore, no mystery and no disease is involved, if suggestion rests on an opening and closing of motor channels which goes on automatically and to a high degree independent of conscious will, if everyone is open to suggestions and yet suggestions are able to turn white into black and black into white, it seems indeed astonishing that the work of justice is carried out in the courts without ever consulting the psychologist and asking him for all the aid which the modern study of suggestion can offer. There is no one participant in the drama of the court who might not change the plot by the operation of suggestions in his mind: the defendant may have worked under suggestion at the time of his criminal deed, the witnesses may be influenced during their observation of the deed or may labour under suggestion on the witness stand and, even if their observation and recollection is correct, their narration may still be tainted by the strange spell; but is the lawyer or the judge, above all, is the juryman less open to a disturbance of the normal ideational rivalry ?

To be sure, popular imagination runs often enough into the

suspicion that a crime was performed under hypnotic influence; but just this is on the whole more a motive for dime novels than for legal consideration. All the probabilities are against it. For the purpose of justice it is far more important to keep in mind that hypnotism is only the strongest degree of suggestibility and that the weaker states of openness for suggestion are the real hotbeds of criminal impulses. We know to-day, for instance, that alcohol poisoning can produce with many persons a state of suggestibility in which complete imitations of post-hypnotic suggestions become possible. The order to do a certain foolish act at an appointed hour in the sober state will be carried out when the order has been given in an impressive way while the wine was still paralysing the inhibitory centres. In the same way emotion changes the man; during a panic the suggestibility is reinforced to a degree where all resistances seem to be broken down, and to be a member of a crowd is always sufficient to weaken the counter action. But there are many persons whose unusual suggestibility makes them constantly liable to chance influences, even in normal social life. They are enthusiastic for the last arguments they hear, and the next speaker who says the opposite convinces them just as fully. The psychological experiment can measure the degree of this constitutional weakness with exactitude, and to leave this nervous disposition altogether out of account in judging the criminal act is in principle not different from punishing the insane like a normal man.

Still more important than the influence of suggestion on the crime is that on the report of the witness. The distortion may begin with the mere perception of the circumstances. Whenever the court becomes doubtful as to whether the witness really observed the facts correctly, we hear some speculative generality as to the probability of a reliable judgment. Here again the first thing ought to be to find the personal equation and to determine by the means of science to what degree the perceptive consciousness of the observer remains independent of intruding suggestions. The suggestible witness may have heard distinct words where the objective witness heard only a noise. Much may depend upon that for the trial. Words distinguished by the unsuggestible mind would count for much; those distinguished by the suggestible one for almost nothing. But to say which is which, it ought not to be sufficient to rely on hearsay and anecdotes, with all the means of the laboratory experts at disposal to determine the exact degree of suggestibility, just as experts would decide whether a bullet can have taken the one way or the other through the body.

Where the perception was fairly correct, the recollection may be entirely distorted by suggestive side influences. We have spoken of the experiments which prove the powerful influence of suggestive questions. No doubt the whole situation of the court-room reinforces the suggestibility of every witness. In much-discussed cases current rumours, and especially the newspapers, have their full share in distorting the real recollections. Everything becomes unintentionally shaped and moulded. The imaginative idea which fits a prejudice, a theory, a suspicion, meets at first the opposition of memory, but slowly it wins in power, and as soon as the suggestibility is increased, the play of ideas under equal conditions ends, and the opposing idea is annihilated. Easy tests could quickly unveil this changed frame of mind and, if such a half hypnotic state of suggestibility has set in, it is no wiser to keep the witness on the stand than if he had emptied a bottle of whiskey in the meantime. And even if the memory itself is correct, the narration may be dictated by suggestive influences and the reported story itself may work backwards with auto-suggestive influence on the memory. There are not a few who finally believe their hunting stories after they have told them repeatedly.

Is it necessary to say that the most suggestible man in the court and the one whose suggestibility is most dangerous may be neither the criminal nor the witness, but the juryman? His task demands freedom from suggestion more than almost any other quality. He has to weigh the value of conflicting evidence. Here again psychological experiment can show how easy it is to interfere with the unhampered play of rival ideas when the mind is suggestible. The lawyer who knows his average juryman instinctively makes the richest use of all the psychological factors which bring the arguments of the one side fully into the focus of interest and suppress and inhibit the effectiveness of the opposite idea. But here again there may be a degree of suggestibility which simply interferes with the purpose of justice and only psychological experiment can bring such deficiency to light. The judgment of a jury becomes a caricature, if not the evidence, but insignificant and accidental circumstances determine the attitude of the suggestible juror.

Of course public opinion with its crowd of instincts is for the most part just such a suggestible arbiter. I heard at the centre of politics that after the Spanish War, when the nation was delighted with the navy and all kinds of scandals seemed to bring evidence against the army, Congress would never have voted so much to the army had not West Point in that year won the football match over Annapolis, and thus swung round the suggestible public opinion from navy to army. But, to be sure, when the Court of public opinion begins to weigh the evidence, it is no longer law, but politics, and it might not be wise to ask how far there is suggestion in politics too, inasmuch as we might be checked too soon by the counter question: Is there anything in politics which is not suggestion?

8
Hypnotism and Crime

Those stubborn people who simply did not believe that such a thing as hypnotism existed have probably now slowly died out; they might just as well have refused to believe that there are mental diseases. And those of the other extreme, those who saw in the hypnotic state a mystical revelation in which superhuman powers manifested themselves, have slowly lost their ground now; they might just as well call sleep or hysteria or epilepsy a supernatural mystery. No, science understands to-day that the facts of hypnotism are in no way more mysterious than all the other functions in the natural life of the mind. They are narrowly related to the experiences of absorbing attention, vivid imagination and obedient will and, on the other side, to sleep and dreams and mental aberration.

Of course, there nevertheless still remains much under heated discussion. There is no real agreement yet as to where the limits of hypnotism lie and where it shades off into suggestion. There are various possible interpretations of the hypnotic brain process, various views also as to the special disposition for it, and even its symptoms still need careful inquiry. But everyone may agree at least in this: that hypnotism is not without serious con-sequences and is therefore certainly not a plaything. And secondly: that hypnotism is for many nervous and mental disorders a highly effective remedy when applied by the experienced physician. It has brought and will bring health and through it, happiness to uncounted sufferers, and therefore it has come to stay.

But if hypnotism is to be with us it seems natural that the question should be asked — often not without anxiety: — What is its relation to law and court, to crime and criminal procedure? The uncanny power which man has therein over men, will over will, suggests the thought that dangerous social entanglements may threaten or that new energies in the interest of the law may be made thereby available. The imagination has here a free field; the dime novel and, alas ! the dollar-and-a-half novel have made full use of this convenient instrument of criminal wonders, and the newspaper public reads, often without any feeling for the difference, stories of hypnotic crime which might easily have taken place by the side of others which are absolutely impossible. There is nowhere a standard, and it may therefore be worth while to take a bird's-eye-view of the whole field in which hypnotism and crime come really or supposedly in contact with each other.

The popular imagination turns first with preference to the query whether the court may not apply hypnotism for the purpose of unveiling the hidden truth. Unsolicited letters concerning hypnotism turn up copiously in a psychologist's mail; statistics show that it is just this proposition which disturbs the largest percentage of these amateur criminologists. They take a passionate interest in every murder case and too often reach the torturing stage of not knowing who is really guilty, even when all evidence and the verdict of the jury is in. Their scruple, they feel, could be removed only by their absolutely knowing that this or that man speaks the truth. Hypnotism has the well-known power of breaking down the resistance of the will; if the hypnotised witness were ordered to speak the full truth, he would no longer have any choice. It looks so simple and promising.

From a purely psychological standpoint such a method might be successful. It is not different in principle from the hypnotic confessions which a patient may make against his will. The other day a student whom I was curing of the cocaine habit assured me most vehemently that he had no cocaine in his room any more, and a few minutes later, when I had hypnotised him, he described correctly the place where he had hidden it. But the difficulty would begin with the fact, too often misunderstood, that one cannot be hypnotised by a new person for the first time against his will. A criminal who does not confess in his full senses will not yield to any hypnotising efforts, as no outsider can bring about the new state of mind. Hypnotisation cannot work on an unyielding brain as a sponge with chloroform which is held by force to the mouth might work. If the imagination of the subject does not help in reaching the somnambulic state, no one can inject a mesmeric fluid into his veins. And finally, even if such hypnotising by force were possible, it is self evident, from moral and legal reasons, that no civilised court ought to listen to such extorted evidence.

Of course, it might be different if a wrongly accused defendant or a suspected witness wished in his own interest to be hypnotised. A woman once asked my advice in such a case. She was under a cloud of ugly suspicion; even her own husband did not believe her protestations of innocence, and, I suppose, her lawyer still less. She wanted to be brought to the deepest state of hypnotism in open court till it would be evident that she had no will-power left for deceit. If she declared herself innocent on the question of the hypnotiser, the court would have to accept it. I advised her strongly not even to suggest such a theatrical performance. Technically, it is not at all possible to hypnotise everyone to such a strong degree, further it would be difficult to prove to the court that she did not simulate hypnotic sleep and that no secret agreement existed between the subject and her hypnotiser. But the decisive point for me was the conviction that the court ought to accept such somnambulic utterances as little as the insane speeches of a paranoiac. She would be no longer in full possession of her mental energies, as it is the essence of the hypnotic state that large parts of the inner functions are inhibited: all is suppressed which counteracts the suggestions of the hypnotiser. She thus would cease to be really herself, and the person on the witness stand would therefore not remain legally the witness who took the oath before the hypnotisation.

Quite different is the case when the hypnotisation is required to awake in the mind the memory of facts which occurred in an earlier hypnotic sitting. It is well known, indeed, that a person awaking from hypnosis may be without any memory of the words spoken, but may remember everything, even months after, as soon as a new hypnotic state is produced. Such a sharpened dream memory may become important, and here the break of personal unity is no hindrance, as the purpose is objective information; for such an end even an insane man may give acceptable evidence, perhaps as to the place where stolen booty is hidden.

But that the court should hypnotise would in any case be a most exceptional event; what is deserving of much more attention is the case when the criminal hypnotises. Here again popular misunderstandings prevail. Here belongs, first of all, the absurd fear of the man with paralysing powers. He enters the room and when he looks on you, you are powerless; you give him your jewels and the key to your safe and he plunders you gently while you have to smile and cannot raise a hand. The English newspapers insisted that such a "burglar with the hypnotic eye" is "the latest product of America." *Punch*, the London Charivari, poked fun at him with a long poem on John P. Beck of Fortieth Street — Was as smart a burglar as one could meet. "On one thing only would he rely — The power of his black hypnotic eye." At first John P. burglarises the halls of the millionaires. Finally he comes before the jury, but every witness begins to talk nonsense as soon as John P. looks at him. "And each who came through the witness door — Seemed still more mad than the man before." And at last he looks on the judge, and the judge, too, begins to get confused and absurd and closes finally: "I know the criminal. Yes, you see — The wretch before you. I am he! — The man who should be in the dock is me! — Arrest me, warders! Step down, John P."

Now all this is, of course, extremely funny, but *Punch* wanted to be still funnier, and therefore introduced, with a serious face, the burlesque poetry with a prose remark. It closes with the statement: "Professor Munsterberg of Harvard and other learned men have set themselves to show that hypnotic power may become a most dangerous asset of the criminal." That is amusing, indeed — because hardly anyone who is interested in the psychology of hypnotic states has sought and used so constantly the chance to ridicule the belief in a special "hypnotic power." I know well that not a few disagree with me in this, but I must insist and have always insisted that anyone can hypnotise anyone.

Of course, whoever wants to hypnotise — in fact, no one but a physician ought to do it — must learn the technique and apply it patiently and skilfully. And certainly there are individual differences. Not everyone can be deeply hypnotised; with not a few the inhibition does not go further than the inability to open the eyes, while only one of four enters into strong hypnotic hallucinations. Further, not everyone is well prepared to awake that confidence which is essential and that feeling of repose which guides one over to the dreamy state; the look, the voice, the gestures, the phrases, the behaviour of certain persons make them poor hypnotisers, however well they may understand the tricks. But in principle everyone can hypnotise and can be hypnotised, just as in principle everyone can love and can be loved and no especial mysterious power is needed to fall in love or to awake love.

Yet, while thus everyone can exert hypnotic influence, no one can do it by a mere glance. All the stories of a secret influence by which one man's will gets hold of another man's mind are remainders of the mesmeric theories of the past. We know to-day that everything depends upon the attention and imagination of the hypnotised and that no mysterious fluid can flow over. This mystical view of unscientific superstition reached its climax in the prevalent belief that a man can exert such a secret influence from a far distance, without the victim's knowledge of the source of the uncanny distortion of his mind. Thus every heinous crime can be committed under that cover. The distant hypnotiser can inflict pain and suffering on his enemy and can misuse the innocent as instrument of his criminal schemes. ·

Such a reappearance of the old witchcraft superstitions is especially characteristic for the borderland cases between normal and abnormal minds. An unsound intellect easily interprets the stray impulses of the mind as the intrusion of a distant adversary. In Germany, for instance, a talented writer bombarded the legislatures with his pamphlets demanding new laws for the punishment of those who produced criminal perversions through telepathic influence. The asylums are full of such ideas. The paranoiacs are always inclined to explain their inner disturbances by the newest startling agencies. Their mind is disturbed by Roentgen rays or wireless telegraphy or hypnotic influence from a distance. In this country such accusations have become familiar to the students of Christian Science. In "Science and Health" Mrs. Eddy wrote, "In coming years the person or mind that hates his neighbour will have no need to traverse his fields, to destroy his flocks and herds . . . for the evil mind will do this through mesmerism; and not in *propria persona* be seen committing the deed." And again, "Mesmerism is practised both with and without manipulation; but the evil deed without a sign is also done by the manipulator and mental mal-practitioner. The secret mental assassin stalks abroad and needs to be branded to be known in what he is doing." Or, "That malicious animal-power seeks to kill his fellow mortals, morally and physically, and then to charge the innocent with his crimes."

There ought to be no compromise: that morally ruinous doctrine of " Malicious Animal Magnetism" is a complete distortion of the facts. Nothing of that kind is ever possible. Some agree that if the surprising facts of hypnotism are possible, such telepathic mesmerism might be possible too, as the influence looks similar. We might just as well propose: if the surprising fact is true that a hen can be hatched from a hen's egg, it may also be true that a hen can come from a white candy egg, as they look alike. It is exactly the essentials of hypnotism and telepathy which are dissimilar and not to be compared: the latter would be a mystery, the former is no harder to explain than any act of sense impression and attention.

Of course, there is no reason to deny that a person may fall into hypnotic state while the hypnotiser is at another place. The only condition is, that he must have been hypnotised by him before and that his own imagination has been captured by the thought of the absent hypnotiser. I myself have repeatedly hypnotised by telephone or even by mail. I treated, for instance, a morphinist who at first came daily to my laboratory to be hypnotised; later it was sufficient to tell him over the telephone: Take your watch out, in two minutes you will fall asleep; or to write to him: As soon as you have read this note, you will be in the hypnotic state. I thus had the "malicious" influence over a distance, but it was not by will power, it was the power of his own imagination; at the time when he read my note in his suburb and fell asleep, I was not thinking of him at all. As a matter of course, such influences by correspondence would have been impossible had not repeated hypnotisation in personal contact preceded. Even that may not be necessary if not complete hypnotisation but only suggestive influence is in question. A few days ago I got a letter from a Southern lady whose son suffers from morphinism. I have never seen either of them. She writes: "My son has been impressed with the belief that your treatment is all he needs to be cured. In a dream, he said, you stood before him with the finger-tips of your hands trembling and said: I have the power to influence your will. He woke repeating: You have the power to control my will. That morning he seemed to forget to take the morphine at the regular time and soon went down to the beach without his morphine outfit in his pocket — an unusual thing," and so forth. He himself was convinced that my will power was working on him while I did not even know him.

The chief factor is confidence. Anyone who saw the hypnotic effects, when the greatest master of hypnotism, Professor Bernheim of Nancy, in France, went from bed to bed in the clinics simply saying: Sleep, sleep, felt that indeed no one else could have attained that influence. But not because he had a special power: the chief point was that the whole population about Nancy went to him with an exaggerated tension of expectancy and confidence. I remember the case of a suffering woman whom I tried at first in vain to hypnotise; I felt that her mind was full of antagonism. I slowly found out what troubled her. She had seen so many physicians who had sent her high bills that she was afraid doctors humbug nervous patients for money. I told her that I, as a psychologist, do such work only in the interest of science, and that I, therefore, as a matter of course, have never accepted a cent from any patient anywhere. Two minutes later she was in deep hypnotic sleep.

The attention and emotion of the subject is thus much more important than the power of the hypnotiser. Yet, this does not exclude the possibility that attention and emotion may be stirred up intentionally, perhaps even maliciously, without conscious knowledge of the victim. There is no especial power which produces love, and yet the coquettish smile of a wilful girl may perturb the peace of any man. In this way a hypnotiser may not wait till the subject lies down with the conscious expectation of being hypnotised, but may work slowly and systematically by means of a hundred little tricks on the imagination of a susceptible person. While both the hypnotic eye which fascinates the first glance and the malicious magnetism from a distance are absurd inventions, such slow and persistent gaining of power over an unresisting mind is certainly possible. A full hypnotic state cannot be reached in such a way; it shades off into the states of submission which belong to our normal social life; there is increased suggestibility in love and fear, in the pupil's feeling towards the teacher and the patient's feeling towards the physician — nowhere a sharp demarcation line between these most valuable influences of social authority and the abnormal suggestions which have their climax in the complete hypnotic state. Such semi-hypnotic state can work, of course, also for good, but the dangers of its misuse are evident.

I remember the tragic case of a young Western woman who seems to have lived for years such a depersonalised social life. She had gone through college and graduate university work and every one of her instructors and comrades was charmed with the lovely girl; but her finest gifts showed themselves in her delightful family life. Her aged mother and her sisters were her only thoughts. The family made the acquaintance of an Italian who posed as a rich Italian count. He was without means, without education, disreputable and mannerless, from the lowest level. The girl was disgusted with him, but he managed to see her often. She felt with aversion how his influence grew on her; she felt a shiver when he looked at her, and yet an uncanny sensation crept over her, a strange fascination which she could not overcome; she had to do what he asked and finally what he ordered her to do. She despised him, and yet one day they secretly left the house and were married. At once he took possession of the young woman's considerable property. But it was not only that she gave him all; under his control she began absurd lawsuits to deprive the family of all they owned; she swore on the witness stand in court to the most cruel accusations and attacks against her mother, who had never wavered in her devoted love for her daughter, and everyone who knew her before felt from her expression and her voice that she was not herself any more, but that she was the passive instrument of an unscrupulous schemer. Her own mother said: "Sometimes, for a few minutes, I seemed to get near her — then she would seem gone, miles and miles away. There are no words to describe the horror of it." And the sister wrote: "I should go crazy if I saw her often." And such a weird spectacle of an elusive mind, which is the old personality and yet not the old self, is not quite rare in our court rooms. It is a hypnotic state which is pregnant with social dangers, but certainly, as said before, there is no fear that it can be brought about suddenly or from a distance; it needs persistent influence, works probably only on neurotic persons with a special disposition for mental inhibitions, and never reaches complete hypnotism.

How far now does the full hypnotic state itself fall within the realm of criminal action? One aspect offers itself at once: the hypnotised person may become the powerless instrument of the criminal will of the hypnotiser. He may press the trigger of the gun, may mix the poison into the food, may steal and forge, and yet the real responsible actor is not the one who commits the crime but the other one who is protected and who directed the deed by hypnotic suggestion. All that has been demonstrated by experiments a hundred times. I perhaps tell the hypnotised man that he is to give poison to the visitor whom I shall call from the next room. I have a sugar powder prepared and assure my man that the powder is arsenic. I throw it into a glass of water before his eyes and then I call the friend from the next room. The hypnotised subject takes the glass and offers it to the newcomer; you see how he hesitates and perhaps trembles, but finally he overcomes his resistance and offers the sugar water which he must take for poison. The possibilities of such secret crimes seem to grow, moreover, in an almost unlimited way through the so-called posthypnotic suggestions. The opportunity to perform unwillingly a crime in the hypnotic sleep itself is in practical life, of course, small and exceptional. But the hypnotiser can give the order to carry out the act at a later time, a few hours or a few days after awaking.

Every experimenter knows that he can make the subject go through a foolish performance long after the hypnosis ended. Go this afternoon at four to your friend, stand before him on one leg and repeat the alphabet. Such a silly order will be carried out to the letter, and only the theoretical question is open, whether the act is done in spite of full consciousness, or whether the subject falls again under the influence of his own imagination at the suggested time into a half hypnotic state. Certainly he does not know before four o'clock that he is expected to do the act, and when the clock strikes four he feels an instinctive desire to run to the house of his friend and to behave as demanded. He will even do it with the feeling of freedom and will associate in his own mind illogical motives to explain to his own satisfaction his perverse desires. He wants to recite the alphabet to his friend because his friend once made a mistake in spelling, Might he not just as well run to his friend's house and shoot him down if a criminal hypnotiser afflicted him with such a murderous suggestion? He would again believe himself to act in freedom and would invent a motive. The situation becomes the more gruesome, as the criminal would have only half done his work in omitting to add the further suggestion that no one else would ever be able to hypnotise him again and that he would entirely forget that he was ever hypnotised. Experiment proves that all this is entirely possible, and that posthypnotic suggestion thus plays in literature a convenient rôle of secret agency for atrocious murder as well as for Trilby's wonderful singing.

In contradiction to all this I have to confess: I have my doubts as to the purity of Trilby's hypnotic singing, and I have more than doubts — yes, I feel practically sure that no real murder has ever been committed by an innocent man under the influence of posthypnotic suggestion. It is true, I have seen men killing with paper daggers and poisoning with white flour and shooting with empty revolvers in the libraries of nerve specialists or in laboratory rooms with doctors sitting by and watching the performance.

But I have never become convinced that there did not remain a background idea of artificiality in the mind of the hypnotised, and that this idea overcame the resistance which would be prohibitive in actual life. To bring an absolute proof of this conviction is hardly possible, as we cannot really kill for experiment's sake.

There remains, of course, also the possible claim that the courts have condemned men for murder for which they were passive instruments. Yet, it is a fact that so far no murder case is known in which the not unusual theory of the hypnotic influence seemed probable after all evidence was in. I have repeatedly received inquiries from lawyers asking whether there would be any basis to stand on if the defence were to claim that the crime was done in a hypnotic or posthypnotic state. I have replied every time that, in spite of the many experiments which seem to prove the contrary, it can be said that hypnotic suggestion is unable to break down the inner resistance. There is therefore no danger to be feared from this side. The frequent claim of defendants that they must have been hypnotised is, nevertheless, mostly no conscious invention. It is rather the outcome of the fact that the criminal impulse comes to the unbalanced diseased mind often like a foreign intruder; it takes hold of the personality without free choice of motives, and the unfortunate sufferer thus interprets quite sincerely his unaccountable perversions as the result of strange outside influences.

But there is another side, and it would be reckless to overlook the difference. You cannot make an honest man steal and kill, but you can make him perform many other actions which are not immoral as far as the action is concerned and which yet have criminal character. The scoundrel perhaps gives the posthypnotic suggestion that his subject, a man of independent means and without immediate relatives, call at a lawyer's and deposit with him a last will leaving all his property to the hypnotiser. Here no resistance from moral principle is involved; the man who throws away all he owns acts in accordance with the order because the impulse is not checked by the habits of a trained conscience. We can add one more step which is entirely possible: the hypnotiser may see a further opportunity to give the posthypnotic suggestion of suicide. The next day the victim is found dead in his room; everything indicates that he took his own life; there is not the least suspicion: and the hypnotiser is his heir in consequence of the spurious last will. Similar cases are reported, and they are not improbable. The easiness with which any hypnotiser can cover the traces of his crime by special suggestions makes the situation the more dangerous.

In this group belong also the posthypnotic perjuries. Of course, if the man on the witness stand knew that he swore falsely, his moral convictions would rebel as in the case of the theft and murder. But he believes what he swears; on his side there is no crime, but merely confusion of ideas and falsified memory; the crime belongs entirely to the one who fabricated the artificial delusion.

In many of these cases the hypnotised subject is the sufferer while he himself is acting; they are not seldom supplemented by crimes in which the subject is a passive sufferer. The French literature of hypnotism is full of cases in which hypnotised women have been the victims of sexual crime. No warning can be loud enough, indeed, against hypnotising by anyone but reliable doctors of medicine. Other cases refer to simple fraud. The posthypnotic suggestion may force one man to pay the price of real pearls for glass pearls and may induce another man to buy a house which is useless for him. The physician who is a trained psychologist will have no difficulty in assisting the court in all such situations and in making the right diagnosis; on the other hand, without thorough experience in scientific psychology, no one will be able to disentangle such cases, be he physician or not. The hypnotiser may have suggested complete forgetfulness and may have prohibited any new hypnotisation, but there always remains somewhere a little opening where the psychologist can insert a wedge and finally break open the whole mental structure. It may be added at once that the psychologist has also no difficulty in recognising any simulation of hypnotic states.

There remains still one important relation between hypnotisation and crime: hypnotisation may prevent crime. The moral interest we take in the suppression of criminal impulses makes us inclined to see a sharp demarcation line between these socially destructive tendencies and other impulses which are morally indifferent. Psychologically we cannot acknowledge such a distinct line between them. The craving for an immoral and illegal end may take possession of a weak nervous system in the same way in which any neurasthenic impulse becomes rooted, and it seems therefore not unjustified to hope for such a criminal disposition the same relief by hypnotic treatment as for the neurasthenic disturbance.

Last year I was approached within the same week by two young people who complained in almost identical terms that they could not master their ideas and desires. The one suffered from the idea that he wanted to kill certain persons; whenever he saw them he felt the impulse to knock them down. The other suffered from the idea that she wanted to look alternatingly from one eye to the other of any person with whom she talked. The impulse to kill was possibly of the greatest consequence, the impulse to look from eye to eye was evidently the most indifferent affair. And yet the second person was the greater sufferer. She had once by chance observed in a man's face a striking difference in colour between his two eyes, and that led her to look alternatingly to the one and the other eye. It became a habit which grew stronger than her will and, when she came to me, it had reached a point where she thought of suicide because life had become intolerable from this incessant impulse to swing from eye to eye. I treated the dangerous killing impulse and the harmless swinging impulse exactly alike, by inhibitory suggestions, and they disappeared under the hypnotic treatment in exactly the same time.

But it is evident that the criminal impulses cannot be simply treated as an appendix to the neurasthenic states. Most complex and partly moral questions are involved therein. Have we a right to reinforce righteousness by hypnotic instead of by an appeal to spiritual energies? If we cure the depraved boy of his stealing habit by hypnotism, would it not be the simple logical consequence that his whole education and training ought to be left to such a safe and forceful influence? And that opens the widest perspective of social problems. It leads us to a new and separate question: What can the modern psychologist contribute to the prevention and suppression of crime ?

9

The Prevention of Crime

A few weeks ago there stumbled into my laboratory a most pitiable human wreck; I saw at the first glance how morphine had devastated the frame of a man in his best years, and trembling and with rolling eyes he confessed that he was using thirty grains of the destructive poison every day. He could neither eat nor sleep, he had not worked for years, he had left wife and child, — it was a gruesome story of heartrending misery. They had sent him to asylums in vain; he remained the slave of his passion, and everyone treated him with contempt and disgust. Slowly I drew out his whole tragedy from the beginning. He had been successful in life and hard at work; then he had had an accident and had been brought into a Southern hospital. There the surgeons gave him morphine every evening to secure a restful night, just a little "shot" of an eighth of a grain. When he left the hospital his hip was healed, but the poor fellow could not sleep without the drug, and from day to day the dose had to be increased — he was a morphinist, an outcast, without energy and without hope.

For weeks I have been fighting his passion with persistent suggestive treatment, and the dose he needs has now been reduced to the hundredth part, and his old strength and enjoyment of life have slowly come back; he will be cured soon. But every day when I put my full energy to the task, I have to think of the cruelty with which society has treated him. He was not born a "dope fiend"; he did not choose the poison. Organised society injected it into his system — a small dose only, but enough to make the craving for it irresistible, and when it had grown to ruinous proportions society was ready to despise and to condemn him. Even in the best case it could only make heroic efforts to overcome the gigantic passion which it had recklessly raised. To me this diseased passion is a symbol of all the crime that fills the countries of the globe. No man is born a criminal. But society gives him without his will the ruinous injection — of course, a small dose only, a shot of an eighth of a grain, and despises him if the injected instinct grows and grows, and when it has destroyed the whole man, then society goes heroically to work with police and court and punishment. It is nearly always too late — to prevent that first reckless injection would have been better than all the labour of the penitentiaries.

At last this conviction is making its way everywhere: prevention of crime is more important than treatment of crime. It is claimed that this country spends annually five hundred million dollars more on fighting the existing crime than on all its works of charity, education and religion; the feeling is at last growing that a fraction of that expense and energy would be ample for providing that such a quantity of habitual crime should not come to existence at all. For such a result, however, it is essential that all social factors coöperate in harmony and that no science which may contribute to this tremendous problem hold back. It is evident that it is the duty of modern experimental psychology to give its serious attention to such thoughts, and a psychologist may therefore ask for a hearing. He has perhaps little to contribute, as only in very recent days has the psychological laboratory come into connection with the world of crime, but that little is the more needed to awake interest for this too much neglected aspect of the case.

Public opinion, to be sure, to-day leans toward calling the

psychologist as witness for a very different purpose. The psychologist is to disburden society of its responsibility for the growth of crime, inasmuch as he is called to testify that the criminal is born as such. Reminiscences of Lombroso's interesting theories and of his whole school fill the air. It seems a dogma that the true scientist must accept the type of the born criminal along with other human abnormalities which are beyond our social making and unmaking, like the epileptic, or, on the sunny side of society, the musical genius. But in such a form the doctrine is certainly misleading and distorted, and the psychologist must refuse to furnish evidence. No one will deny the importance of those Italian inquiries which were quickly amplified by the researchers of all countries. It was of the highest value to study the bodily and mental characteristics of the inmates of our prisons, to gather anthropological and sociological data of their misshapen ears or palates, of their tattooing and their slang, and finally to make psychological experiments as to their sensitiveness and their emotions. But no result justifies the claim that criminals are born as such. The accusation against society stands after Lombroso firmer than before; society has not done its duty.

From the outset we must not forget that from a psychological point of view it is utterly vague to speak of a criminal disposition as if such a term stood for a unified mental state. In the old days of reckless phrenology it seemed so simple to talk of the sense for architecture or the sense for morality, and in the same way of the absence of such sense, as if really one elementary function only were involved. All that was necessary for the old phrenologist, because it was his belief that he was able to recognise the development of mental functions like love of music or criminality from the development of certain bumps on the skull; and for that purpose it was again necessary to presuppose that such mental traits were located in one single corner of the brain. To-day we know that such faculties are the outcome of hundreds of thousands of processes which are going on in perhaps millions of brain parts. We may seek the localised seat for simple tone sensations or simple colour sensations, but not for a whole perception of a thing, and infinitely less for such complex states, built up from ideas, emotions, and volitions.

How does the average man succeed in living an honest life? Impressions and thoughts carry to his mind numberless ideas which awake feelings of pleasure and displeasure. The pleasurable idea stirs up the desire and the impulse to realise it in action, and the disagreeable idea awakes the impulse to get rid of the displeasing source. There is no further will act necessary; the idea, of the end itself presses the brain button and makes us act. We approach the attractive and escape the painful by the mere power of the ideas; the whole development of life from the first sucking for sweet milk is possible only through this mechanism. But from the beginning life complicates this process. The tempting idea of the end to be reached awakes, before the action sets in, some counter idea, perhaps the thought of dangerous results; we desire the fruit, but we know it is poisonous, and the idea of poisoning works in the opposite direction. The attractive impression gives the impulse to extend the arm, and the thought of danger gives the counter impulse to withdraw the arm. The one tends to inhibit the other; the more vivid idea overpowers the weaker one; we do not grasp for the poisonous fruit, because the danger holds as back.

Such counter idea, which associates itself with the idea of the end, may be of social character; the expectation of punishment or of contempt may work as such a check, and yet the mechanism of the process is just the same. It is again a balancing of opposing forces. And finally, instead of such social ideas, there may stand on the other side a religious habit or an ethical ideal which may become effective where no social fear is involved, but the principle remains always the same: the struggle of ideas controls the resulting action. There is no good or bad, wise or foolish actor behind those ideas to pick out the favoured one, but the ideas in their varieties of vividness and feeling-tone with their attached impulses are themselves the working of the personality, and their striving determines the result. A life may be honest, or at least decent, if the tempting ideas of socially forbidden ends are inhibited and over-powered by opposing considerations, ideas of punishment and harm, or of religious fear. On a higher level we may demand that it shall be the idea of moral dignity which checks the forbidden impulse. But the essential point remains that the non-criminal, the correct life, is always the result of a complex interplay between ideas and counter ideas with the result that the thought of some unpleasant consequence inhibits the desire. The mechanism of the process is therefore not different from the case where the idea of bodily harm prevents us from doing a reckless or dangerous thing. And in this way the psychologist cannot acknowledge a special function of non-criminal behaviour; it overlaps and practically coincides with the reasonable, cautious way of living in every other respect. By the smallest possible steps every man's adjustment to his environment leads from the avoidance of bodily risks to the avoidance of social risks, and thus to non-criminal habits. There is nowhere a sharp demarcation line. The one who is instinctively overmuch afraid of being found out in wrong-doing will live a faultless life from the standpoint of law; just as truly as his neighbour who obeys the laws from a moral conviction. It is impossible to bring criminality, from a psychological viewpoint, down to one formula.

The normal decent life thus demands that an idea which by its feeling tone stimulates to a forbidden action shall awake, at the same time, the counter ideas which stimulate to the inhibition of the action, and that these opposing ideas shall remain victorious. It is evident that crime may thus result from most different reasons. Those social counter ideas may not have been learned, or they may not come quickly enough to consciousness, or they may be too faint, or, on the other hand, the original ideas with their desires may be too intense, or their emotions may be too vehement, or the mechanism of inhibition may not be working normally — in short, a defect or an abnormality in any part of the complex process may lead to a conflict with the law. And yet how different the mind in which the impulses are too strong from that in which the opposing ideas are too faint and that in which the inhibition does not work precisely. And where is to be the point at which the defect becomes abnormal? The temperament with strong impulses may remain still quite well behaved if the checking ideas are unusually strong too, and the faint checks may be harmless if the desires are still weaker.

Moreover, it is clear that none of these defects works in the direction of crime alone. The brain in which such counter ideas are too slowly associated has no special trouble in the line of legal consequence alone; it is a general deficiency; all the ideas come slowly, the mental vision is narrow; the man is stupid and mentally lazy. On the other hand, the brain in which the opposing ideas are unable to produce inhibition must do the reckless thing everywhere: he runs risks and does not care. And the brain in which the impulses are overstrong will again show its emotional lack of balance in every field. In short, there are minds which are born slow or stupid or brutal or excitable or lazy or quaint or reckless or dull — and in every one of such minds a certain chance for crime is given. But to be born with a mind which by its special stupidity or carelessness or vehemence gives to crime an easier foothold than the average mind certainly does not mean to be a born criminal. The world is full of badly balanced or badly associating persons; we cannot deny that nature provided them poorly in the struggle for social existence; they are less fit than others, but their ending within prison walls is only one of the many dangers which life has in store for them; the same unfit apparatus may make them unable to gain a position or to have friends or to protect themselves against disease. In short, it is not criminals that are "born," but men with poorly working minds. And yet who will say where a mind is just of the right kind? No brain works perfectly — what intelligence and what temperament would be ideal? "All the world is peculiar." It is thus only a question of relative amount.

Just this, indeed, is the situation which the psychologist finds. Of course, if we turn to the professional criminal who has become a specialist at safe-blowing or at sneak-thieving or at check-forging or burglary, and who has been shaped by long years in the penitentiaries, we find specimens of mind which are very different from the normal average; but those are the differences of training. They have become indeed almost unable to avoid crimes; they have to go on in their career, but it was not their inborn disposition that forced them to burglary. If we abstract from the effect of such life training in the social underworld, and from the traces of poor education, of bad example, of disease and neglect, we find among the criminals the same types of mind as in other spheres, only with a great percentage of all kinds of mental inferiority — stupid and narrow minds, vehement and passionate minds, minds with weak power of comprehension and minds with ineffective power of inhibition, minds without normal emotions and minds without energy for work.

When a school for criminal boys was carefully examined, it was found that of the two hundred boys one hundred and twenty-seven were deficient in their general make-up, either in the direction of feeble-mindedness or in the direction of hysteric emotion or in the direction of epileptic disturbance. And fuller light is thrown on these figures as soon as others are added; in eighty-five cases the father or the mother, or both, were drunkards; in twenty-four cases, the parents were insane; in twenty-six cases, epileptics; and in twenty-six further cases, suffering from other nervous diseases. Not the criminal tendency was born with the poor children, but the insufficient capacity and resistance of the central nervous system; and this was their inheritance from abnormal and degenerate parents.

If we wish to express it in terms of experimental psychology, we may consult the careful tests which have been made with female criminals in Southern penitentiaries, on the one side, and female students of a large university on the other. Certainly, point for point the criminals show a different result. For instance, in memory tests the average student remembered a series of seven letters or a series of eight numerals, while under the same experimental conditions the average criminal remembered only five letters or six numerals. Or the test for the attention to tactual impressions showed that the students discriminated two compass points as two on the right fore-arm at a distance of sixteen millimetres, while the criminals did not discriminate them with less than twenty-four millimetres. If students pulled at a hook as fast as they could, their energy would be decreased in half a minute by 1.6 pounds, while that of the criminals decreased by 2.4 pounds. Or if a word was given as starting point for any associations which might arise in consciousness, the average number of associations in one minute was for the students ten, for the criminals five. In short, in every respect the average of the criminals shows a poorer mental equipment than the average of the picked student minds. But here again no one feature points to a special demand for crime. Criminals are recruited especially from the mentally inferior; that is the only true core of the doctrine of the born criminal. But the mental inferiority — intellectual or emotional or volitional — forces no one to steal and burglarise. He cannot and will never equal the clever, well-balanced, energetic fellow, but society may find a modest place, humble but safe, even for the most stupid and most indifferent and most unenergetic: no one is predestined by his brain to the penitentiary.

It may be replied, of course, that there are plenty of cases in which crime is committed from an irresistible impulse or from a total lack of inhibition or from other defects which exclude free self-determination. But in such cases we have clearly no longer any right to speak of crime; it is insanity. The man who starts incendiary fires because he has hallucinations in which he hears God's voice ordering him to burn the town, is not a criminal. Moreover, the pathological impulses of the diseased mind are again not confined to the criminal sphere; again crime is only the chance effect; the disturbance is general. The irresistible impulse may be just as well directed against the man's own personality, and may lead to self-mutilation or to suicide. And that holds true also for the milder degrees. Only to-day I studied the case of a lad of eleven who was brought to me because he was found stealing from time to time. He was a dear little boy, surrounded with comfort and the best and most loving influences. He fights and fights against his impulse and speaks of it frankly. Sometimes it comes like an attack; he longs for some money perhaps to buy fire-crackers with, and he simply cannot resist till it is done, he told me with tears, and then he hardly knows why he did it. But it was evident at the first glance that the boy was not normally built, and that the attacks which led to such pseudo-crimes were pathological, quite similar to epileptic or hysteric fits. To prevent such explosions of the diseased brain is not prevention of crime; but, on the one side, treatment of disease, on the other side, protection of society against the outbreaks of dangerous patients. In real crime we have to presuppose that the checking of the impulse by the counter idea would have been possible if the available energy had been brought into play. Crime is thus not a disease, and there is no need to excuse the existence of our jails by considering them as asylums. Every action is, of course, the necessary result of foregoing causes, but such effect of the causes remains a free, and therefore a responsible action, as long as the causes work on a mechanism which is able to secure an unhampered interplay of influences. The insane or the hypnotised mind has no freedom and therefore cannot commit crime, but the merely stupid or reckless or brutal or indifferent minds are still free, while it is clear that the probability of a disastrous result is for them alarmingly high.

If we thus exclude the pathological mind from further discussion, we can say that no one is born a criminal: what, then, has society to do that no one shall become a criminal? The latest of all sciences, eugenics, might look backwards and demand that society take care that such mentally weak and inferior persons are not born at all. Vital statistics show indeed on some of their darkest pages that the overwhelming majority of those degenerate personalities have drunkards and epileptics as parents. But our immediate lack is a different one: we presuppose that the minds of the millions in all their variations of strong and weak, of intelligence and emotionality and power are born and sent into the streets of the cities; what can the psychologist advise that their way may not lead them from the street to the cell of the prison?

But now the problem has become simplified. We know the mechanism which keeps men straight; we can foresee, therefore, what influences must be detrimental. If the counter idea is to balance and to overcome the first desire, we can foresee that the chances for crime must grow if the impulses are strengthened or if the counter ideas are weakened or eliminated, or if the inhibitory apparatus is damaged, or if in any other way the sound balance is tampered with. Here is indeed the place for the experiment of the psychologist. He can isolate the special factors and study their influence under the exact conditions of the laboratory. We may take illustrations at random.

We said that crime involves an impulse to action which is normally to be checked. The checking will be the more difficult the stronger the impulse. The psychologist therefore asks: What influences have the power to reinforce the impulse? Has, for instance, imitation such an influence? Mere speculation cannot answer such a question, and even so-called practical experience may lead to very mistaken conclusions. But the laboratory experiment can tell the story in distinct figures. I ask my subjects, for instance, to make rhythmical finger movements by which a weight is lifted, and the apparatus in which the arm rests records exactly the amount of every contraction. After a while the energy seems exhausted; my idea has no longer the power to lift the weight more than a few millimetres; the recorded curve sinks nearly to zero. I try with encouraging words or with harsh command; the motor energies of these word-stimuli are not ineffective; the curve shows a slight upward movement, but again it sinks rapidly. And then I make the same rhythmical movement myself before the eyes of my subject; he sees it and at once the curve ascends with unexpected strength. The movements have now simply to imitate the watched ones, and this consciousness of imitation has reinforced the energy of the impulse beyond any point which his own will could have reached. It is as if the imitation of the suggestive sight suddenly brings to work all the stored-up powers. The psychologist can vary the experiment in a hundred forms; always the same result, that the impressive demonstration of an action gives to the impulse of the imitating mind the maximum of force — it must then be the one condition under which it is most difficult to inhibit the impulse. How many helpful suggestions for the good, for education and training and self-development can be drawn from such facts; but, much more, how many warnings against the reckless fostering of criminality! In millions of copies the vulgar newspaper pictures of crime reach the homes of the suggestible masses and every impulse towards the forbidden is dangerously reinforced. Every brutality spreads outward and accentuates the lawless impulses in the surrounding; the abolition of prize fights and whipping posts is not enough.

To point in another direction: everything must be fatal for weak honesty which reduces the power of restraint. The psychological experiment can here analyse the influences, for instance, of our usual stimulants — coffee and tea, tobacco and alcohol, drugs and nervina. Laboratory experiment indicates perhaps only slight variations in the rapidity of movements in the memory tests or in the discriminations of stimuli, but every one of those changes must be endlessly magnified if it is projected into the dimensions of a world-city in which the millions indulge in artificial excitement and stimulation. Take the well-studied case of alcohol. We ask, let us say, a number of normal men to go through a series of experiments in their ordinary state.

We may begin with a reaction time experiment. That means we study how long it takes to make the quickest possible hand-movement in response to a flash-light or to a click; we measure the time between the light or sound stimulus and the reaction in thousandths of a second. Then we vary it by a test where various movements are to be made in response to different lights, so that a choice and discrimination is involved. We then turn, perhaps, to memory experiments — with the learning of letters or figures or words. Next may be an experiment in intellectual activity; we measure the time of simple arithmetical operations. Then we study the mental associations; for instance, we give a list of two hundred words and our subject has to speak for each one the first word which flashes on his mind. We may then study the character of these closely-bound ideas and may group them statistically. Then we measure with a dynamometer the strength of the greatest possible effort for action. Next in order perhaps we study the judgment of our subject in his estimation of space and time distances, then the accuracy with which he imitates a given rhythm, then the rapidity with which he counts the letters of a page, then the sharpness of attention with which he discriminates a set of short impressions, and so on through other tests for other mental functions. For every test we get his average figures. And then we begin the examination of the effect of the stimulants. How are all these exactly measurable functions changed twenty minutes or an hour or two hours after taking a dose of one ounce or two ounces or three ounces of pure alcohol, whiskey, beer or champagne?

Only such a variety of tests gives the possibility of disengaging the effect and of understanding where the real disturbance sets in. Certain functions seem certainly improved. For instance, we soon find that the reaction time test gives smaller figures under alcohol, at least in a first stage; the subject who needs normally, say 150 thousandths of a second to press a telegraph key after hearing a click, may need only 125 thousandths of a second half an hour after his alcohol dose. But is that really an improvement? The same records show that while the time of the reaction decreases there appear at the same time wrong reactions which did not occur in his normal state; again and again, the key is pressed before the signal is really heard, the impulse explodes when any chance touches it off instead of remaining under the control of consciousness which waits for the click.

In the same way, it seems in the first short period from the dynamometric tests that the alcohol brings an improvement of motor energy, but half an hour later the tables are turned, the muscular effectiveness is decreased. In the field of associations the time of bringing a new idea to consciousness becomes longer, the process is retarded, but, more important, the associative process becomes more mechanical. If we call those associations external in which an idea awakes another with which it is connected in space or time, and internal those which involve a thorough relation, a connection by meaning and purpose, we can say that the external associations strongly increase with alcohol and the internal ones become eliminated. Still greater are the changes in mechanical memorising, which is at first greatly facilitated and in calculation, which suffers from the first. The strongest improvement is shown in reading, the greatest difficulty in the intellectual connection.

And if the various threads are connected by careful study, we get a unified result: all motor reactions have become easier, all acts of apperception worse, the whole ideational interplay has suffered, the inhibitions are reduced, the merely mechanical superficial connections control the mind, and the intellectual processes are slow. Is it necessary to demonstrate that every one of these changes favours crime? The counter ideas awake too slowly, hasty action results from the first impulse before it can be checked, the inhibition of the forbidden deed becomes ineffective, the desire for rash vehement movements becomes overwhelming. In such a way experimental psychology can carry the vague impressions of the bystander into a field of exact studies where mere prejudices are not allowed to interfere, but where real objections can be substantiated. Moreover, the general statements can be particularised by subtler examinations still: how does alcohol work in different climates, at different seasons, at different hours of the day, in work and in fatigue, in different states of health, with food and without, for different ages, different sexes, different races, and how is the effect of pure alcohol related to that of the various beverages, to whiskey and beer and wine? Only if we can differentiate the mental influences through such experimental tests can we secure a rational protection against one of the most persistent sources of social evils.

With the same methods we might study tobacco and coffee and tea, bromides and morphine, but also the effects of physical or mental overstrain, of bad air and bad light, of irrational nourishment and insufficient sleep, of exhaustive sports and emotional exertions, and a hundred other factors which enter into the daily life of the masses. On such an experimental basis only can we hope for regulation and improvement; a sweeping proscription, of course, might be reached without laboratory studies: simply to forbid everything is easy, but such radicalism is practically impossible as far as the evidence of fatigue or poverty is concerned, and perhaps possible but unwise as far as the stimulants are in question. The psychological experiment must show the middle way which shall close the fountains of evil and yet keep open the sources of good.

Mere abstinence from stimulants, indeed, is no real solution of the problem; it is just the psychologist who knows too well the evil effects of monotony and emptiness; who understands that the craving for stimulants and artificial excitement belongs to the deepest conditions of our physical existence, and that the complete suppression of it leads to mental explosions which bring man again to disastrous impulses and crime. The laboratory experiment can demonstrate in turn how the psychological conditions are changed when such a dreary state of waiting and monotony lays hold on the mind; how certain mental functions are starving and others dangerously overwrought. A state of dullness and expectant attention is created in which the longing for contrast may intensify the desires to a point where the reaction is more vehement than under any stimulant. That is the state which, projected into the masses, may lead to gambling and perversity, and on to irrational crimes, which through the mere excitement of the imagination overcome the emptiness of an unstimulated life.

Or the experiment may undertake to examine the subtler mechanism of mental inhibition: how far does the suppression and inhibition of the motor impulse depend on the intensity of the counter stimulus and how far on habit — that is, on unbroken repetition? How is it altered by interruption of training or by the feeling-tone of the ideas? Simple measurement of reaction times may be again the method, varied by the introduction of warning signals which are to counterbalance the stimulus. Yet the short schematic experiments of the psychologist's workshop illustrate clearly how and why a public state of lawless corruption and general disrespect of law must undermine the inhibitory effects of the law and thus bring crime to a rich harvest. That is just the wonderful power of the psychological experiment, that it can analyse the largest social movements in the smallest and most schematic miniature copies of the mental forces involved, and from the subtle analysis is only one step to the elimination of dangers. What the commercialism of our time or the vices of the street, the recklessness of the masses and the vulgarity of the newspapers, the frivolity of the stage and the excitement of the gambling halls may mean for the weak individual cannot be better understood than through the microscopical model of it in the experimental test which allows subtle variations.

The psychologist will thus certainly not believe that all or most is done for the prevention of crime by mere threatening with punishment. The question, in this connection, is not whether the punishment satisfies our demand for retaliation or whether the punishment helps indirectly towards prevention by educating and reforming the man behind whom the doors of the penitentiary are closed. The question is now only whether the fear of a future judicial punishment will be a sufficient counter idea to check the criminal impulse. The psychologist cannot forget that too many conditions must frustrate such expectations. The hope of escaping justice in the concrete case will easily have a stronger feeling tone than the opposing fear of the abstract general law. The strength of the forbidden desire will narrow the circle of associations and eliminate the idea of the probable consequences. The stupid mind will not link the correct expectations, the slow mind will bring the check too late when the deed is done, the vehement mind will overrule the energies of inhibition, the emotional mind will be more moved by the anticipated immediate pleasure than by the thought of a later suffering. And all this will be reinforced if overstrain has destroyed, the nervous balance or if stimulants have smoothed the path of motor discharge. If the severity of cruel punishments has brutalised the mind, the threat will be as ineffective as if the mildness of the punishment had reduced its pain. And, worst of all, this fear will be ruled out if the mind develops in an atmosphere of crime where the child hears of the criminal as hero and looks at jail as an ordinary affair, troublesome only as most factors in his slum life are troublesome; or if the anarchy of corruption or class justice, of reckless legislation or public indifference to law defeats the inhibiting counter idea of punishment and deprives it of its emotional strength. The system of punishment will be the more disappointing the more mechanical it is in its application. The plan of probation thus means a real progress.

More important than the motives of fear are the influences which can shape the minds of the tempted, the influences which reduce the emotional and motor powers of forbidden desires, awake regularly and strongly the social counter ideas, strengthen their inhibiting influence, and weaken thus the primary impulse. It must be said again: criminals are not born, but made — not even self-made, but fellow-made. Society must work negatively to remove those influences which work in the opposite direction. The atmosphere of criminality, the vulgarity and brutality, the meanness and frivolity of the surroundings must be removed from the mind in its development. And if the social contrasts are necessary for much of the good, at least the vulgar esteem of mere riches and the pitiless contempt for misery can be eliminated. Above all, a well-behaved mind grows only in a well-treated body; true, far-seeing hygiene can prevent more crime than any law. But it is not only a question of the favourite work of our hygienists, the infectious and germ diseases, together with the sanitary conditions of factories and tenements. Hygiene has to take no less care of the overworked or wrongly treated senses and nerve systems from the schoolroom to the stock exchange; there is no gain if we avoid typhoid epidemics but fall into epidemics of insanity. The whole rhythm of life breaks down the instruments of nervous resistance, and the most immediate symptom is necessarily the growth of crime. It is not the impulse itself, but the inability to resist the impulse that is the real criminal feature. The banker who speculates with the funds of his bank is not a criminal because such an idea arises in his consciousness, but because his idea is not inhibited by the counter ideas, and yet the whole community has pushed to break down the barriers which his mind could have put into the motor path of the ruinous impulse.

Of course, the negative precautions must be supplemented by the positive ones. Hygiene has not only to destroy the unclean, but to build up the clean. And for mental hygiene this holds still more strongly. To create a public life which is an example and an inspiration to the humblest, which fills with civic pride the lowest, — means to abolish the penitentiaries. The public welfare must give to everybody through work, through politics, through education, through art, through religion, a kind of life interest and life content in which envy is meaningless. It is from this realm that the counter ideas must be reinforced that automatically check the impulse to the immoral deed. But no public scheme can make superfluous those clearest sources of pure life, the motives of private personal interest between human being and human being. Everything which strengthens family life and works against its dissolution, everything which gives the touch of personal sympathy to the forlorn, helps towards the prevention of crime. How often can a criminal life be fundamentally changed as soon as the absurd prejudice is given up that every criminal is a different kind of man from those outside of jail, and straightforward sympathy instead of mere charitable pity is offered. To make them feel that they are recognised as equals means to win them over to decency. And those who analyse them psychologically know well that there is really no condescension necessary for such acknowledgment. They are the equals of the unpunished; they are stupid or lazy or vehement or reckless or uneducated or unemotional or egotistic, but all that we find on this side of the legal demarcation line as well. We are accustomed to bow to the stupid and lazy and reckless and egotistic, in case that life has brought them under conditions where a sufficient balance was secured; they are not different in their inmost selves, even if surroundings, bad example, overwhelming temptation, the saloon, the cruelty of misfortune has once in a hasty hour destroyed that balance.

There lies finally the deep importance of a full confession. The man who confesses puts himself again on an equal ground with the honest majority; he belongs again to those who want both health and justice; he gives up his identity with the criminal and eliminates the crime like a foreign body from his life. A true confession wins the bedrock of life again and is the safest prevention of further crime. The psychologist — I say it with hesitation, as my observations on that point may not yet be complete enough, and the subject is an entirely new one — may even be able to find out by his experiments whether a true confession is probable or not.

After all, the actions of every man strive for satisfaction, and there cannot be satisfaction without unity. He who lives in the present only gains such satisfaction from the immediate experience; the pleasure and enjoyment of the present hour is the end of his consciousness and absorbs him so fully that complete unity of mind is reached. Another type rushes forward, the mind directed toward the future; the suffering of the hour is overborne by the hope of the coming success, and present and future complete for him the unity of life. Both those who turn to the present and to the future cannot have a desire for true liberating confession. But it is different with those who have a vivid memory and whose mind is thus ever turning back to the past. There is the unending conflict between their memories which belong to the life of purity, to childhood and parents' love, to religion and friendship, and the present sorrow and anxiety; the craving for unity must end this struggle; a confession connects the present with the past again and throws out the interfering intrusion of shame. If the experiment of the psychologist demonstrates the possession of a vivid living memory, the chances are strong that a confession is to be trusted. The criminal deed is thus almost a split-off consciousness, a part of a dissociated personality, and through the confession it is cut off absolutely. On the other hand, if it is too late, if the split-off part has grown to be the stronger and has finally become the real self, then it is nearly always too late for prevention by social hygiene; the criminal who has become a professional is nearly always lost, and society has only to consider how to protect itself against the damage he is effecting. He must be separated from the commonwealth just as the insane must be removed from the market places of life. Short punishment for the professional criminal is useless and harmful in every respect. But his career is a terrible warning against delaying the prevention of crime till society — rashly ignoring psychology — has itself manufactured the hopeless criminal.

LaVergne, TN USA
07 April 2010
178502LV00007B/142/P